READING BULLETIN BOARDS ACTIVITIES KIT

JERRY J. MALLETT

Illustrated by Mark D. Smith

THE CENTER FOR APPLIED RESEARCH IN EDUCATION
West Nyack, New York 10994

Library of Congress Cataloging-in-Publication Data

Mallett, Jerry, J.
    Reading bulletin boards activities kit/Jerry J. Mallett;
illustrated by Mark D. Smith
      p.   cm.
    ISBN 0–87628–692–9
    1. Readings—Aids and devices.   2. Reading (Elementary)
3. Bulletin boards. I. Smith, Mark D. II. Title. III. Title:
Reading bulletin boards activities kit.
LB 1573.39.M35 1988
  372.4—dc19   87-21484
                                        CIP

© 1998 *by* The Center for Applied Research in Education

Printed in the United States of America

10 9 8 7 6 5 4 3 2 1

ISBN 0-87628-138-2

To Sue Beth Arnold . . .
an outstanding teacher and good friend
                            JJM

To Phyllis Ann Stover-Smith . . .
a super educator and understanding wife
                            MDS

**THE CENTER FOR APPLIED RESEARCH
IN EDUCATION**
West Nyack, NY 10994
A Simon & Schuster Company

On the World Wide Web at http://www.phdirect.com

Prentice Hall International (UK) Limited, *London*
Prentice Hall of Australia Pty. Limited, *Sydney*
Prentice Hall Canada, Inc., *Toronto*
Prentice Hall Hispanoamericana, S.A., *Mexico*
Prentice Hall of India Private Limited, *New Delhi*
Prentice Hall of Japan, Inc., *Tokyo*
Simon & Schuster Asia Pte. Ltd., *Singapore*
Editora Prentice Hall do Brasil, Ltda., *Rio de Janeiro*

About the Author

Jerry J. Mallett has been actively involved in elementary education for more than 25 years, as a classroom teacher, reading specialist, school principal, and professor. Awarded his doctorate by the University of Toledo in 1972, he is presently Professor of Education at Findlay College, Findlay, Ohio.

Dr. Mallett is the author of many articles on reading instruction and is also the author of *Classroom Reading Games Activities Kit, 101 Make-and-Play Reading Games for the Intermediate Grades, Library Skills Activities Kit,* a five-unit series of *Library Skills Activity Puzzles,* and the *Elementary School Library Resource Kit.*

About the Illustrator

Mark D. Smith has 15 years' experience as a professional artist and illustrator, during which time he has illustrated over ten books for children. Mr. Smith has been an art educator for 12 years at the secondary level with the Findlay (Ohio) City Schools. He received his B.A. degree from Bowling Green State University.

About This Kit

The *Reading Bulletin Boards Activities Kit* has two primary purposes: to help you expand children's interest in reading and to help you reinforce specific reading skills. For easy use in selecting appropriate displays, the *Kit* is organized into two sections: Motivation Builders and Skills Builders. The Skills Builders section is then divided into the following skills areas:

- classification/relationships
- sight word knowledge
- initial consonants
- final consonants
- medial vowels
- consonant blends
- contractions
- compound words
- synonyms and antonyms
- context clue usage
- main ideas
- important details
- sequence of events

Each skills section contains a lesson plan with which to introduce the particular skill to the students and at least four bulletin boards or displays designed for skill reinforcement. In all, more than 75 bulletin boards and displays are included in this book.

As a further aid to you, all materials are printed in a large 8½" x 11" format. Where appropriate, answer keys are included for quick checking of children's work by you or by the children themselves. In addition, there are many full-size patterns you can copy in making the bulletin boards and displays.

You will find that the *Reading Bulletin Boards Activities Kit:*

- helps you motivate children to explore and read a wide variety of books
- offers a practical and simple way to stimulate children to do the necessary drill of reading skills
- utilizes simple, commonplace materials normally found in most classrooms and libraries
- is especially helpful in sparking initiative in reluctant readers
- includes bulletin boards and displays to help children learn 13 specific reading skills

The *Reading Bulletin Boards Activities Kit* will provide a continuing, year-round source of practical bulletin boards to enrich, revitalize, and reinforce all aspects of your reading program.

Jerry J. Mallett

Contents

About This Kit... iv

MOTIVATION BUILDERS...................................... 1

Find Me the PURRRfect Book • 2
Try for the Tastiest • 2
Ezra Jack Keats Favorite! • 9
Rita's Readers • 12
Poetry Popcorn Problem • 15
Attack Those Books! • 18
Round Up a Reading Partner • 22
Soar Into Reading • 22
Don't Read These in the Dark! • 28
Jungle Jive! • 32
Roscoe's Riddles • 32
Jack and the Beanstalk • 37
No More DOG-gone Excuses . . . Read • 40
Get in the Swim with Selsam • 43
Smile! • 46
A Wheelbarrow of Wordless Books • 49
The Family Tree • 51
And the Dish Ran Away with the Spoon • 53
Super School Stories • 56
Reading Is a Life Preserver! • 58
Going Bananas over Reading • 62
Books You Can't *BEAR* to Put Down! • 62
Books for a Rainy Day • 66
Reading Is Terrif<u>egg</u>! • 69

SKILLS BUILDERS.. 71

Classification/Relationships

Introductory Lesson • 72
Bulletin Boards and Displays
    Sylvia the Sea Monster • 76
    Pick a Pocket • 79

Hang It Up • 81
Inside or Outside • 83

Sight Word Knowledge

Introductory Lesson • 85
Bulletin Boards and Displays
Let's Play Badminton • 89
Pick a Pair • 91
Wagon of Words • 94
Wordopolis • 96

Initial Consonants

Introductory Lesson • 99
Bulletin Boards and Displays
Pirate Pickworth's Pistol • 103
Consonant Curtains • 106
Cheeta Swings • 110
Karl's Quiet Corner • 112

Final Consonants

Introductory Lesson • 115

Bulletin Boards and Displays

Help Bert Mail the Letters • 119
Plant a Posy • 122
Lots of Lollypops • 125
Crazy Caboose • 128

Medial Vowels

Introductory Lesson • 131
Bulletin Boards and Displays
Deep-Sea Diver • 135
Sip a Soda • 138
Ride the Big Wheel • 140
Rough Sea • 142

Consonant Blends

Introductory Lesson • 145
Bulletin Boards and Displays
    I Vont You! • 150
    Bucket of Blends • 153
    Spin-A-Blend • 156
    Dangerous Dive • 158

Contractions

Introductory Lesson • 160
Bulletin Boards and Displays
    Twig Twirl • 167
    Three-Alarm Fire • 169
    Arnold the Armadillo • 172
    Crocodile Contractions • 175

Compound Words

Introductory Lesson • 178
Bulletin Boards and Displays
    Fly Away • 184
    A Famous Flag • 188
    Compound Equations • 191
    Dr. Grimenstein . . . the Mad Scientist • 193

Synonyms and Antonyms

Introductory Lesson • 195
Bulletin Boards and Displays
    Ladybug, Fly Away Home! • 200
    Andre's Antonyms • 202
    From the Planet Gorgi • 206
    Eloise Goes to the Circus • 208

Context Clue Usage

Introductory Lesson • 211
Bulletin Boards and Displays
    Poochie Pal • 216
    WITCH Is Correct? • 219

Whooo Did It? • 221
Vicious Volcano • 225

Main Ideas

Introductory Lesson • 228
Bulletin Boards and Displays
    The Spider's Web • 233
    Circus Parade Mobile • 236
    Unlock the Doors • 238
    The Main Idea Niche • 240

Important Details

Introductory Lesson • 242
Bulletin Boards and Displays
    Bertrum Bunny • 247
    A DEVIL of a Time! • 250
    Cupboard Confusion • 254
    Snowy Cove • 257

Sequence of Events

Introductory Lesson • 260
Bulletin Boards and Displays
    A Log of Frogs • 266
    Up, Up, and Away! • 269
    A Fine Catch • 273
    Story Frame • 276

Motivation Builders

The bulletin boards and displays in this section are designed to encourage children to read. Each example includes a list of materials needed to construct the bulletin board/display. The sizes of these items will depend on your space available. You will also find simple directions for constructing each bulletin board.

FIND ME THE PURRRFECT BOOK!

Materials Needed:

> yellow background paper
> gray construction paper
> small gelatin or pudding boxes
> stapler
> scissors
> glue
> felt-tipped pen
> 2 ditto boxes

Construction Directions:

1. Use an opaque projector to trace the lettering on the background paper.
2. Cut a cat out of the gray construction paper by using an enlargement of the cat pattern shown in the bulletin board illustration.
3. Attach the cat to the board with the small gelatin boxes as backing for a three-dimensional effect. Staple the boxes to the board and then glue the cat to these boxes.
4. Cut the two ditto boxes in half across the width, cover with gray paper, print "PURRRfect Book Sheets" on the front of one and "Finished Book Sheets" on the front of the other. Attach both to the board.
5. Make copies of the "PURRRfect Book Sheets," and place a supply in the bulletin board box.

Bulletin Board Use:

The children are to take a sheet and draw a book jacket of one of their favorite books. When finished, they are to return the sheet so you may display it on the bulletin board.

TRY FOR THE TASTIEST!

Materials Needed:

> posterboard
> construction paper (various colors)
> felt-tipped pens (various colors)
> paper hole punch
> scissors
> glue

Name _____

Date _____

FIND ME
THE PURRRFECT BOOK!

Help Cleo make the "purrrfect book board." Draw a book jacket for one of your favorite books. When you are finished place it in the "Finished Book Sheets" box. It will be placed on the bulletin board so others may read about your favorite book!

Title _____

Author _____

Find me the PURRRFECT BOOK!

Finished Book Sheets

Directions:

1. Take a "PURRRfect Book Sheet" and fill it in.

2. After you fill it in place it in the finished sheet holder.

3. You will soon find it on this board.

PURRR-FECT book sheeTs

string
Caldecott Honor books
large manila envelope
duplicating master

Construction Directions:

1. Cut and mark the posterboard using an enlargement of the following pattern. Attach the envelope as shown.

2. Cut another piece of posterboard and attach to the figure as shown here.

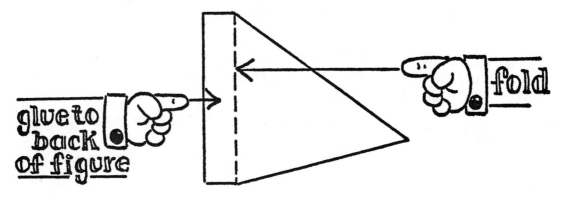

3. Cut and mark the construction paper using the book pattern **shown** here. You will need eight.

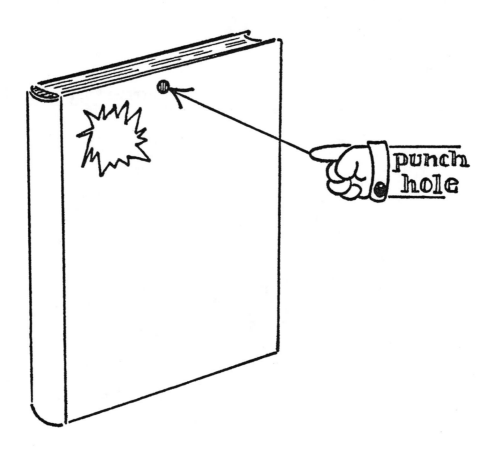

4. Print the following title-author pairs, each on both sides of a different book:

   Frederick by Leo Lionni

   Seashore Story by Taro Yashima

   Goggles by Ezra Jack Keats

   Thy Friend, Obadiah by Brinton Turkle

   The Judge by Harve Zemach

   The Angry Moon by William Sleator

   Frog and Toad Are Friends by Arnold Lobel

   When Clay Sings by Byrd Baylor

5. Suspend the books from the ceiling so they hang around the poster-board figure.

6. Duplicate the "Try For The Tastiest" activity sheet and place a supply in the envelope.

7. Place a small rug in front of the posterboard figure. Choose numerous books from the following Caldecott Honor books to place in the display area:

Andy and the Lion by James Daugherty

Madeline by Ludwig Bemmelmans

April's Kittens by Clare Turlay Newberry

Paddle-to-the-Sea by Holling Clancy Holling

Pedro, the Angel of Olvera Street by Leo Politi

Stone Soup by Marcia Brown

McElligot's Pool by Dr. Seuss

Blueberries for Sal by Robert McCloskey

Juanita by Leo Politi

Bartholomew and the Oobleck by Dr. Seuss

Dick Whittington and His Cat by Marcia Brown

If I Ran the Zoo by Dr. Seuss

Bear Party by William Pene du Bois

One Morning in Maine by Robert McCloskey

The Storm Book by Charlotte Zolotow

Journey Cake, Ho! by Ruth Sawyer

Play With Me by Marie Hall Ets

Crow Boy by Taro Yashima

Anatole and the Cat by Eve Titus

Lion by William Pene du Bois

What Do You Say, Dear? by Sesyle Joslin

Umbrella by Taro Yashima

Houses from the Sea by Alice Goudey

The Moon Jumpers by Janice May Udry

Inch by Inch by Leo Lionni

The Fox Went Out on a Chilly Night by Peter Spier

Little Bear's Visit by Else Minarik

Mr. Rabbit and the Lovely Present by Charlotte Zolotow

Swimmy by Leo Lionni

The Wave by Margaret Hodges

A Pocketful of Cricket by Rebecca Caudill

Hide and Seek Fog by Alvin Tresselt

Hildilid's Night by Cheli Duran Ryan

Name _____

Date _____

TRY FOR THE TASTIEST!

Read two of the books in this display. Draw a
picture of the one you liked best.

Now tell why you liked it best! _____

_____

_____

_____

_____

_____

Anansi the Spider: A Tale from the Ashanti by Gerald McDermott
Strega Nona by Tomie De Paola
The Amazing Bone by William Steig
The Contest by Nonny Hogrogian
Hawk, I'm Your Brother by Byrd Baylor
It Could Always Be Worse: A Yiddish Folk Tale by Margot Zemach
Freight Train by Donald Crews
Ben's Trumpet by Rachel Isadora
The Garden of Abdul Gasazi by Chris Van Allsburg

Display Use:

Point out the display to the children and encourage a discussion of the hungry bookworm. Ask questions such as "What does the term bookworm mean?" "If we called someone a bookworm, what are we really saying about the person?" "You are to 'try for the tastiest' when you read the two books. What does this mean? Why do you suppose the word *tastiest* is used rather than *best*?" Make sure the children understand the connection between the bookworm, the use of "tastiest," and the books they will be reading.

The children are now to read two of the books and then complete a "Try for the Tastiest" activity sheet.

EZRA JACK KEATS FAVORITE!

Materials Needed:

white background paper
felt-tipped pens (various colors)
ditto box
scissors
red construction paper
ditto master
ditto paper
stapler
tape
shoe box

Construction Directions:

1. Use an opaque projector to trace the figures and lettering onto the background paper.
2. Cut the ditto box in half across the width, cover it with red paper, print the word "Ballots" on the front and attach it to the board.

OFFICIAL EZRA JACK KEATS BALLOT

Directions: Place an "X" in the box next to the title of your favorite Ezra Jack Keats book.

☐	*Whistle for Willie*	☐	*A Letter to Amy*
☐	*The Snowy Day*	☐	*Kitten for a Day*
☐	*Goggles*	☐	*Little Drummer Boy*
☐	*Pet Show!*	☐	*Louie*
☐	*Hi, Cat!*	☐	*Louie's Search*
☐	*Apt. 3*	☐	*Maggie and the Pirate*
☐	*Dreams*	☐	*Skates!*
☐	*Peter's Chair*	☐	*The Trip*
☐	*Jennie's Hat*	☐	*John Henry: An American Legend*
☐	*Clementina's Cactus*		

EZRA JACK KEATS FAVORITE!

Directions:

1. Take a ballot and vote for an Ezra Jack Keats book.

2. Fold the ballot and place it in the ballot box.

3. Make copies of the "Official Ezra Jack Keats Ballot" sheets and place a supply in the bulletin board box.
4. Cover the shoe box with red paper and cut a large slit through the top. Print "Ballot Box" on it and place it near the bulletin board.

Bulletin Board Use:

Encourage the children to discuss the bulletin board. Be sure to clarify the voting concept and procedure by explaining the "Official Ezra Jack Keats Ballot," and the "Ballot Box." The children take a ballot and vote for their favorite book.

> SUGGESTION: The bulletin board display should go up several weeks before the voting. Allow only a few days for the voting and post the winner after the ballots are counted.

RITA'S READERS

Materials Needed:

white background paper
scissors
felt-tipped pens (various colors)
ditto master
ditto paper (various colors)

Construction Directions:

1. Use an opaque projector to trace the lettering and figures onto the background paper. Use appropriate colors.
2. Make copies of Rita and the certificate and keep for future use. Use a variety of colors.

Bulletin Board Use:

The children are to keep a list of all the books they read during a designated time span. At the end of this time, these lists are turned in to you. You fill in a Rita reading certificate for each child. Return the sheets and have the children cut out the figures and attach them to the board.

> SUGGESTION: You might keep track of the total books your class reads during one week and then try to improve this figure the second week.

RITA'S READERS

POETRY POPCORN PROBLEM

Materials Needed:

large clear plastic container with lid
popcorn kernels
posterboard
felt-tipped pens (various colors)
scissors
large manila envelope
tape
chair
ditto master
ditto paper

Construction Directions:

1. Cut and mark the posterboard as shown on the bulletin board illustration.

2. Count the kernels of popcorn and place them in the clear plastic container. Tape the lid on!

3. Duplicate the "Petunia Penguin" sheet and place a supply in the envelope.

4. Attach the envelope, poster, and container on a chair as shown here.

5. Set a couple of books on the chair around the container. Here are a few suggestions: *I Met a Man* by John Ciardi, *Ghost Poems* by Daisy Wallace and *Garbage Delight* by Dennis Lee.

Poetry Popcorn Problem

Read a book of poetry and fill out a "Petunia Penguin" sheet. Now you may have one guess as to the number of popcorn kernels in this container. Write it on the sheet and turn it in. Wait for the winner results!

Of yes . . . when you read another book of poetry, you may have another guess!

PETUNIA PENGUIN

Name _____

Date _____

Petunia Penguin just loves poetry so tell her all about the poems you just read.

Book Title _____

_____

Author _____

Tell her the titles of your three favorite poems in the book you just read.

_____

_____

_____

She wants to know why you liked these best.

_____

_____

_____

_____

Now she wants you to close your eyes and think about one of these poems. Which part did you think about? Draw a picture showing something about this favorite part.

popcorn
guess

ATTACK THOSE BOOKS!

Materials Needed:

tan background paper
felt-tipped pens (various colors)
ditto box
white posterboard
scissors
yellow construction paper
2" x 36" cloth strips (white, green, yellow, brown, black)

tape
stapler
small gelatin or pudding boxes
glue
ditto master

Construction Directions:

1. Use an opaque projector to trace the lettering onto the background paper.
2. Cut the karate figure out of the posterboard by using an enlargement of the figure shown in the bulletin board illustration.
3. Attach the karate figure to the board with the small gelatin boxes as backing for a three-dimensional effect. Staple the boxes to the board and then glue the figure to these boxes.
4. Cut the ditto box in half across the width, cover with yellow paper, print "Get a *KICK* Out of Reading" on the front and attach it to the board.
5. Make copies of the "Get a *KICK* Out of Reading" sheets and place a supply in the bulletin board box.
6. Make copies of the karate figure sheet. Make copies on white, green, yellow, brown, and gray (in place of black) paper.

   ALTERNATIVE: You can make all copies on white paper and simply outline the figures and color the belts in the various colors using felt-tipped pens.

Bulletin Board Use:

Read the bulletin board to the students and explain the process of acquiring both karate figure name cards to go on the board and the karate belts. Each time a child fills in one of the "Get a *KICK* Out of Reading" sheets he or she moves up to the next color belt level. At this time you will place the appropriate color name card on the board and "loan" the appropriate color belt to the child.

   SUGGESTION: Children could wear the appropriate belt around school only on the day they reach that level. This will cut down on the number of belts you will need to provide.

ATTACK Those Books

Directions:

1. Take a "Get a *KICK* Out of Reading" sheet and fill it in. You must read three books to complete it!

2. Hand it to your teacher. Each time you do this you will move up to a different color karate belt!

3. See if you can make it all the way to the black belt!!!

Get a
KICK
out of
Reading

Belts books

white	3
green	6
yellow	9
brown	12
black	15

Name _____

Date _____

GET A *KICK*
OUT OF READING

(1) My first book is _____

_____ by _____

The part I liked best is _____

_____

_____

_____

_____

_____

_____

(2) My second book is _____ by _____

_____. If I could change something in this story it would be

_____

because _____

_____

_____

(3) My third book is _____ by _____

_____. The character I liked best is _____

I liked this character because _____

_____

Something I didn't like about the book is _____

_____

_____

ROUND UP A READING PARTNER

Materials Needed:

white background paper   ditto masters
felt-tipped pens (various colors)   scissors
thick rope made from hemp   stapler
straight pins

Construction Directions:

1. Use an opaque projector to trace the figures and lettering onto the background paper. Use appropriate colors.
2. Attach the hemp rope, using the straight pins, as shown.
3. Make copies of both the "Roundup Form," and the "Lasso Name Tag."

Bulletin Board Use:

As children return the "Roundup Forms" to you, print their names on the lasso name tags and attach at the appropriate places around the lasso. As their number increases, move the name tags around the bulletin board lasso. Once they have moved around this lasso they may keep their name tag lasso.

SUGGESTION: You may want to pin this lasso on them to wear around school and home that day.

SOAR INTO READING

Materials Needed:

white background paper   ditto paper
felt-tipped pens (various colors)   scissors
construction paper (various colors)   tape
ditto box   stapler
ditto master

Construction Directions:

1. Trace the lettering and figures on the background paper.
2. Cut the ditto box in half (widthwise), cover with blue construction paper, print "Soar into Reading Sheets" on the front, and attach it to the board.
3. Put copies of the "Soar into Reading Sheet" in the box.

ROUNDUP FORM

_____ and
(student)

_____ do hereby state
(partner)

that we read the following books together during the week of

_____

_____ by _____

_____ by _____

_____ by _____

_____ by _____

_____ by _____

ROUND UP A READING PARTNER!

Directions:

1. Take a "Roundup Form" along with some good books home with you.

2. Then "Round Up a Reading Partner!" Spend some time reading together.

3. Fill in the "Roundup Form" and return. Your name lasso will be placed on the board next to the number of books read.

4. Continue to do this with different reading partners. Your name lasso will be moved each time.

5. See if you can make it all the way around the lasso!

1 2 3 4 5 6 7 8 9 10 11 12 13 14 15 16 17 18 19 20 21

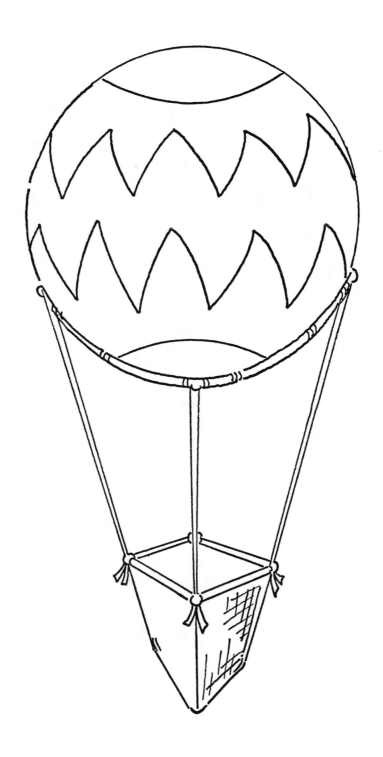

SOAR INTO READING

Directions:

1. Read a book.
2. Fill out a "Soar into Reading Sheet."
3. Give it to your teacher.
4. Hooray! Now you get a Soar into Reading balloon!

Soar into Reading Sheets

SOAR INTO READING SHEET

Name _____

Date _____

I'll draw my favorite part of the book inside the balloon.

Book _____

Author _____

4. Cut and mark the construction paper using the balloon pattern. Attach a few of these to the board as shown in the bulletin board illustration. Keep the remainder in your desk, ready to give to the students.

Bulletin Board Use:

The children take a sheet and draw a picture of something from a book that they have just read. When they are finished, they return the sheets so that you may give them a "Soar into Reading Balloon."

> SUGGESTION: Young children will love to have the balloons pinned to their clothing to wear around school.

DON'T READ THESE IN THE DARK!

Materials Needed:

white background paper	ditto box
black construction paper	ditto master
gray construction paper	ditto paper
straight pins	stapler
felt-tipped pens in various colors	tape
scissors	

Construction Directions:

1. Using an opaque projector, copy the lettering and figures on the background paper. Use appropriate colors.
2. Cut out the letters from the black construction paper and attach them to the bulletin board. You may use the letter patterns provided or use other appropriate patterns. Attach these to the bulletin board using the straight pins. Pull the letters away from the bulletin board to the heads of the pins. This will give a three-dimensional effect.
3. Cut the ditto box in half (widthwise), cover with the gray construction paper, print "Not in the Dark" on the front, and attach it to the board.
4. Make copies of the "Not in the Dark Sheet" and place a supply in the bulletin board box.

Bulletin Board Use:

The children must read a mystery book or a scary story and fill in one of the sheets. Each child who does this may add something to the bulletin board. Just watch the scene expand as the month progresses!

Not in the Dark!

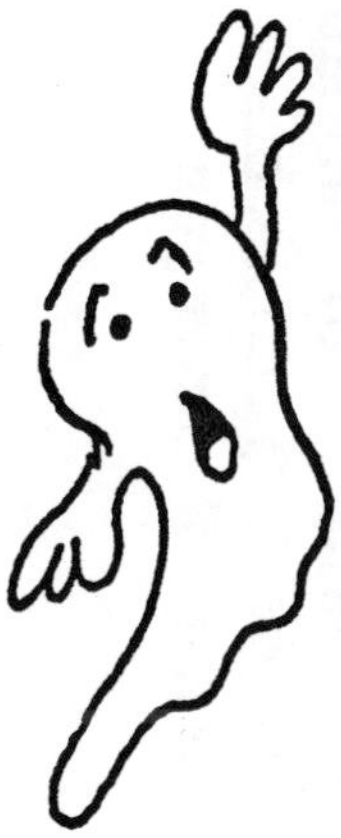

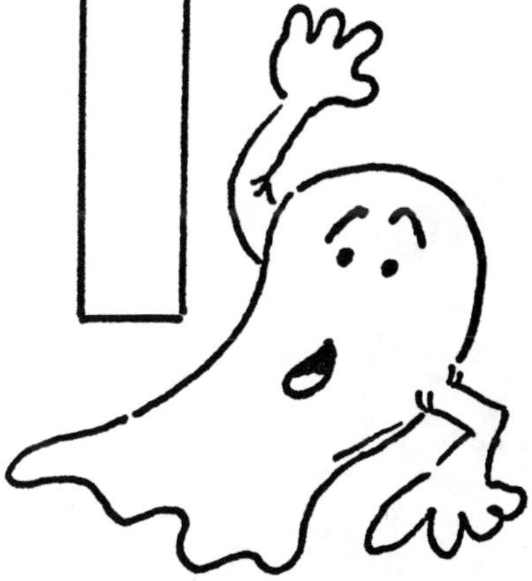

Not in the DARK!

Directions:

1. Read a mystery, a ghost story, or a scary story.
2. Fill in a sheet and give it to your teacher.
3. Now you may add one thing to the haunted cemetery. It can be anything: ghosts, black cats, witches, clouds, bats, or whatever you wish.

Not in the Dark!

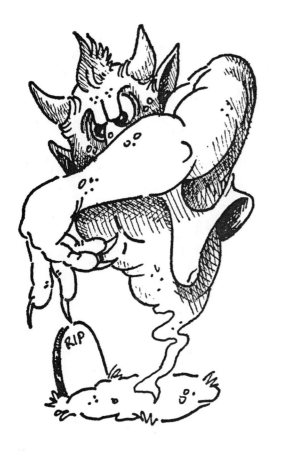

Name _____

Date _____

NOT IN THE DARK

I read the book:

_____

It was written by:

_____

It is about:

_____

_____

_____

The scariest thing in the story is:

_____

_____

_____

Here is a drawing of one of my favorite characters in the story.

JUNGLE JIVE!

Materials Needed:

white background paper
felt-tipped pens (various colors)
green corrugated paper
brown butcher paper
yellow construction paper
white posterboard
scissors
straight pins
stapler
glue

Construction Directions:

1. Use an opaque projector to trace the tree trunk on the brown butcher paper. Attach it to the board.
2. Cut the green corrugated paper as shown in the illustration and attach it with straight pins to give a three-dimensional effect.
3. Cut out letters from the yellow construction paper using the letter patterns and glue to the green corrugated paper as shown in the illustration.
4. Use an opaque projector to trace the animals and lettering on the background paper.
5. Cut out the cartoon speech bubbles from the white posterboard, copy the lettering on each, and attach them to the board.

Bulletin Board Use:

This bulletin board may be used to stimulate interest in reading during a special time, such as Children's Book Week.

ROSCOE'S RIDDLES

Materials Needed:

white background paper
felt-tipped pens (various colors)
ditto box
scissors

Juggling elv

ROSCOE'S RIDDLES

Directions:

1. Take a sheet and make up a riddle about one of your favorite story characters. Then draw a picture of him or her.

2. Give it to your teacher. Your sheet will be placed on the "Roscoe's Riddles" board.

Roscoe's Riddle Sheets

Name _____

Date _____

Directions:

1. Think about one of your favorite story characters.
2. Make up a riddle telling a little about him or her. (Look on the board if you need help.)
3. Now, draw a picture of him or her.
4. Take this sheet to your teacher when you are finished.

Riddle:

_____

_____

_____

_____

_____

_____

_____

Who am I?
This is a picture of the character.

stapler
tape
ditto master
ditto paper
yellow construction paper

Construction Directions:

1. Use an opaque projector to trace the lettering and figures onto the background paper. Use appropriate colors for the rabbit.
2. Cut the ditto box in half (widthwise), cover with yellow construction paper, print "Roscoe's Riddle Sheets" on the front, and attach it to the board.
3. Make copies of the "Roscoe's Riddle Sheet" and place a supply in the bulletin board box.
4. Fill out two of the sheets and attach them to the board as examples.

Bulletin Board Use:

The children take a sheet and make up a riddle about one of their favorite story characters. They also draw a picture of this character. When they are finished, they return the sheet so that you may attach it to the bulletin board.

JACK AND THE BEANSTALK

Materials Needed:

white background paper
felt-tipped pens (various colors)
green construction paper
ditto box
ditto master
green ditto paper
scissors
tape
stapler

Construction Directions:

1. Use an opaque projector to trace the lettering and figures onto the background paper.
2. Cut the ditto box in half (widthwise), cover with green construction paper, print "Beanstalk Leaves" on the front, and attach it to the board.
3. Put copies of the "Beanstalk Leaf Sheet" in the bulletin board box.

JACK
AND THE
BEANSTALK

Directions:

1. Read a book.
2. Fill out one of the leaves and give it to your teacher.
3. It will help the beanstalk grow.

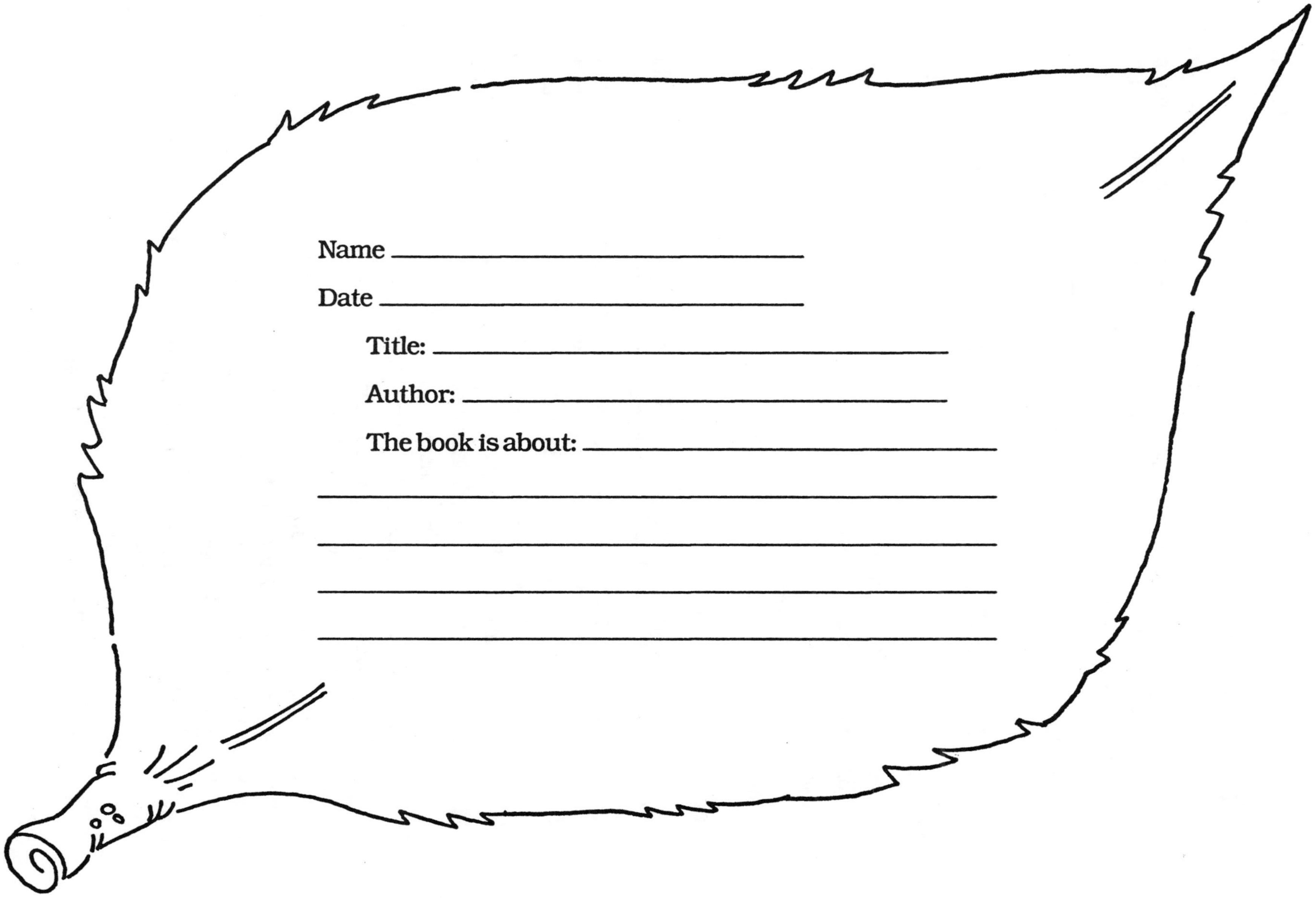

Name _____

Date _____

Title: _____

Author: _____

The book is about: _____

Bulletin Board Use:

The children take a sheet, cut out the leaf, and fill it out. When they are finished, they return the leaf so that you may attach it to the board. Begin at the bottom of the beanstalk and build upward. See how many leaves can be added to the beanstalk.

NOTE: Don't let the size of your bulletin board stop the growth of the beanstalk. Continue taping leaves right up the wall!

NO MORE DOG-GONE EXCUSES . . . READ

Materials Needed:

white background paper
brown construction paper
straight pins
felt-tipped pens (various colors)
scissors

Construction Directions:

1. Use an opaque projector to trace the lettering and figures onto the background paper. Use appropriate colors for the dogs.
2. Using the pattern, cut out dog collars from the brown construction paper. Mount these on the board as shown in the illustration. Attach these with straight pins. Then pull the paper away from the board toward the pinheads. This will give a three-dimensional effect.
3. Select several of the following and copy each within a different collar:
   Bobo's Dream by Martha Alexander
   The Last Puppy by Frank Asch
   Clifford's Good Deeds by Norman Bridwell
   Noisy Book by Margaret Wise Brown
   Henry and Ribsy by Beverly Cleary
   Ribsy by Beverly Cleary
   Angus and the Ducks by Marjorie Flack
   A Bag Full of Pups by Dick Gackenbach
   Barkley by Syd Hoff
   The Biggest, Meanest, Ugliest Dog in the Whole Wide World by Rebecca C. Jones
   Pinkerton Behave by Steven Kellogg
   A Rose for Pinkerton by Steven Kellogg

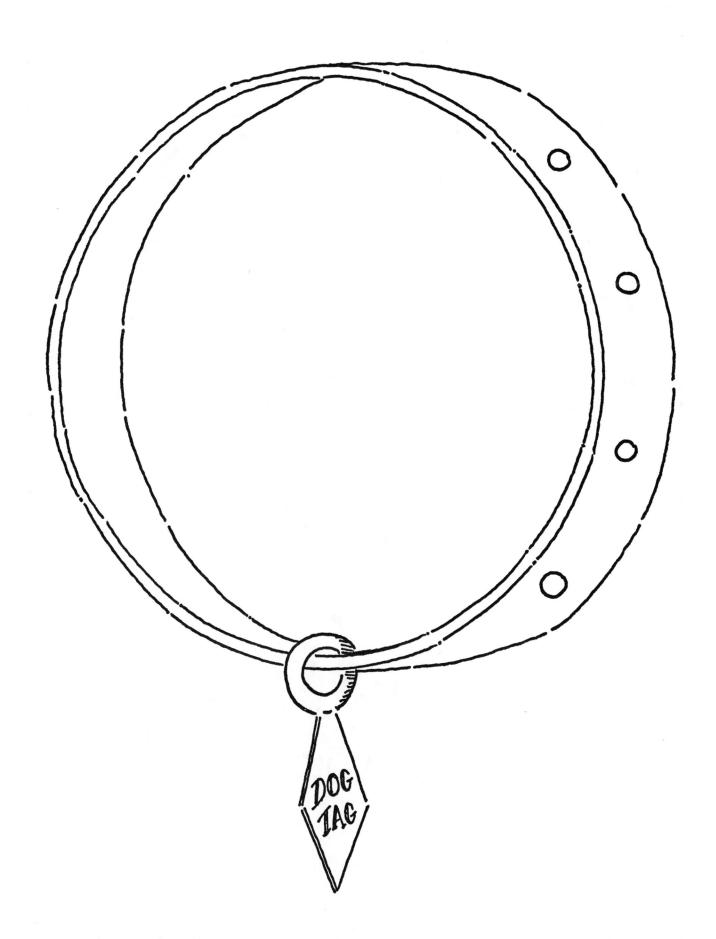

No More Dog-gone Excuses
READ!!!...

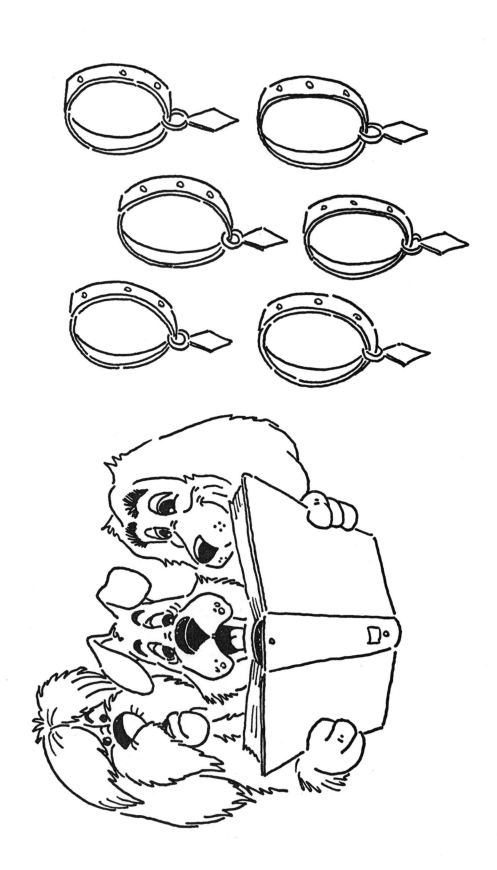

Somebody's Dog by Miska Miles

Barkis by Clare Newberry

Cissy, the Pup by Ruth Odor

Poofy Loves Company by Nancy Winslow Parker

His Mother's Dog by Liesel Moak Skorpen

Old Arthur by Liesel Moak Skorpen

The Housekeeper's Dog by Jerry Smath

Caleb and Kate by William Steig

The Sky Dog by Brinton Turkle

The Garden of Adbul Gasazi by Chris Van Allsburg

Bernard by Bernard Waber

IMPORTANT: Use the names of the books that are available to your children either in your classroom or your school library.

Bulletin Board Use:

The bulletin board may be used to stimulate children's interest in books about dogs.

GET IN THE SWIM WITH SELSAM

Materials Needed:

one small inflatable swimming pool

construction paper

scissors

tape

felt-tipped pens (various colors)

books by Millicent Selsam

Construction Directions:

1. Cut and mark the title words from the construction paper to form "Get in the Swim with Selsam." Tape these to the outside of the swimming pool.

2. Place many books by Millicent Selsam in the pool. Here are some you may choose to use:

The Amazing Dandelion	*Bulbs, Corn, and Such*
Benny's Animals	*Greg's Microscope*
Birth of a Forest	*The Harlequin Moth*
Birth of an Island	*How Kittens Grow*

Land of the Giant Tortoise   *A First Look at Fish*
Popcorn   *A First Look at Insects*
Questions and Answers about Horses   *A First Look at Leaves*
The Tiger   *A First Look at Mammals*
Tyrannosaurus Rex

Display Use:

The children climb into the pool and leisurely read a Selsam book.

CAUTION: One or two "swimmers" only. You may wish to set a time limit for any one swimmer!

SMILE!

Materials Needed:

large cardboard box   ditto paper
chair   construction paper
self-stick vinyl   scissors
large manila envelope   glue
ditto master   a self-developing camera

Construction Directions:

1. Cut the cardboard box as shown here.

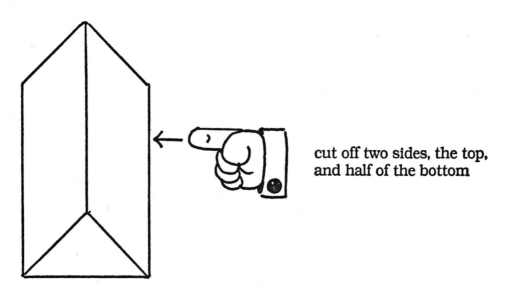

cut off two sides, the top, and half of the bottom

2. Cover the inside with bright self-stick vinyl and place a chair in it.

3. Mark and cut construction paper, as shown here, and attach it to the wall.

Read a humorous book and then fill out one of the sheets.

And then in a FLASH . . . you will be added to our display!

Don't forget to smile!

4. Mark the front of the manila envelope with "Smile Sheets" and attach to a display wall.

Name _____

Date _____

SMILE SHEET

This book, _____

_____

is funny! It was written by _____

_____

The funniest thing that happens in the story

is _____

_____

_____

_____

_____

_____

_____

Here is a picture of something else funny that happens.

5. Duplicate copies of the "Smile Sheet" and place a supply of them in the envelope.

Display Use:

After students have satisfactorily completed the reporting forms, have them each sit on the chair in the display, take their photos (holding the book they have just read), and allow them to attach the photos to the display.

> NOTE: The reporting form sheets should also be attached next to their photos for additional interest builders.

A WHEELBARROW OF WORDLESS BOOKS

Materials Needed:

a toy wheelbarrow

construction paper

felt-tipped pens (various colors)

scissors

tape

wordless picture books

Construction Directions:

1. Place the wheelbarrow next to a wall.

2. Cut and mark the construction paper using an enlargement of the following pattern.

3. Attach the sign on the wall next to the wheelbarrow.

4. Place a variety of wordless picture books in and around the wheelbarrow. The following are examples of books you may want to use:

The Adventures of Paddy Pork by John Goodall

Ah-Choo! by Mercer Mayer

Apples by Nonny Hogrogian

April Fools by Fernando Krahn

A Birthday Wish by Ed Emberley

Bobo's Dream by Martha Alexander

A Boy, a Dog, and a Frog by Mercer Mayer

Catch That Car by Fernando Krahn

Changes, Changes by Pat Hutchins

Creepy Castle by John Goodall

Deep in the Forest by Brinton Turkle

The Great Ape by Fernando Krahn

The Hunter and the Animals by Tomie de Paola

Look What I Can Do by Jose Aruego

Noah's Ark by Peter Spier

One Frog Too Many by Mercer Mayer

Out! Out! Out! by Martha Alexander

Paddy Finds a Job by John Goodall

Pancakes for Breakfast by Tomie de Paola

Peter Spier's Christmas by Peter Spier

Peter Spier's Rain by Peter Spier

Rosie's Walk by Pat Hutchins

The Scribble Monster by Jack Kent

Sebastian and the Mushroom by Fernanda Krahn

The Silver Pony by Lynd Ward

Skates by Ezra Jack Keats

The Snowman by Raymond Briggs

The Sticky Child by Malcolm Bird

Truck by Donald Crews

Two Moral Tales by Mercer Mayer

Up and Up by Shirley Hughes

The Wrong Side of the Bed by Edward Ardizzone

Display Use:

This display may be used to stimulate children's interest in humorous books.

ALTERNATIVE: If you feel in a rather daring mood, you may want to substitute a real wheelbarrow for the toy one. Place it in a corner of your room, fill with pillows and books, and encourage the children to climb in!

THE FAMILY TREE

Materials Needed:

brown corrugated paper   tape or pins
stapler   black felt-tipped pen
scissors

Construction Directions:

1. Staple together a triple roll of corrugated paper to form the tree trunk and tape or pin to a corner as shown in this bird's-eye view.

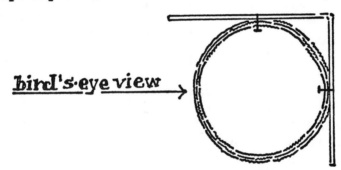

bird's-eye view →

2. Cut and mark the tree trunk as shown in the illustration.
3. Set biographical books around the foot of the tree that are appropriate for your children. Here is a list of biographies written for the primary grades:

   The Columbus Story by Alice Dalgliesh

   The One Bad Thing About Father by Ferdinand Monjo

   Christopher Columbus by Clara Ingram Judson

   Pocahontas by Patricia Miles Martin

   Daniel Boone by Patricia Miles Martin

   Squanto, Friend of the Pilgrims by Clyde Robert Bulla

   Song of St. Francis by Clyde Robert Bulla

   Lincoln's Birthday by Clyde Robert Bulla

The Family Tree

read these books about famous people

look for others in the 920's

Cut a hole in the large tree trunk. Roll a piece of corrugated paper to the size of the hole. Insert this "branch" into the hole and tape it to the trunk.

Washington's Birthday by Clyde Robert Bulla
A Weed Is a Flower by Aliki Brandenburg
The Story of Johnny Appleseed by Aliki Brandenburg
The Story of William Penn by Aliki Brandenburg
Abraham Lincoln by Ingri & Edgar Parin d'Aulaire
Maria Tallchief by Tobi Tobias
Marian Anderson by Tobi Tobias
Arthur Mitchell by Tobi Tobias
Meet Benjamin Franklin by Maggi Scarf
The Story of Ben Franklin by Eve Merriam
Meet Andrew Jackson by Ormonde De Kay
The Picture Life of Martin Luther King, Jr. by Margaret B. Young
Gordon Parks by Midge Turk
Cesar Chavez by Ruth Franchere
Rosa Parks by Eloise Greenfield
Bobby Orr by Marshall and Sue Burchard
Phil Esposito by Marshall and Sue Burchard
Billie Jean King by Marshall and Sue Burchard
Henry Aaron by Marshall and Sue Burchard
Langston Hughes, American Poet by Alice Walker
James Weldon Johnson by Ophelia Egypt
Eleanor Roosevelt by Jane Goodsell
The Ringling Brothers by Molly Cone

AND THE DISH RAN AWAY WITH THE SPOON

Materials Needed:

yellow background paper
white posterboard
10 white paper plates
3 small gelatin or pudding boxes
black felt-tipped pen
scissors
library-book card pockets
legal-size envelope
white construction paper
stapler
glue

Construction Directions:

1. Cut a large spoon out of the white posterboard by using an enlargement of the spoon pattern shown here. Attach the spoon with the small gelatin boxes as backing for a three-dimensional effect. Staple the boxes to the board and then glue the spoon to these boxes.

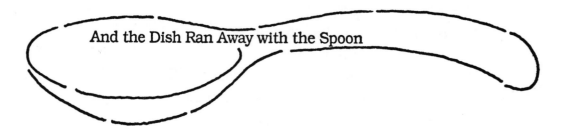

And the Dish Ran Away with the Spoon

2. Attach the paper plates and library-book card pockets as shown in the board illustration.
3. Use an opaque projector to trace the lettering and the figures as shown.
4. Cut the white posterboard using the following spoon pattern.

So What?

5. Write each of the following titles on a different spoon:
   So What?
   The Sign on Rosie's Door
   Carousel
   Peter's Chair
   The Caterpillar and the Polliwog
   The Bicycle Man
   Bernard
   A Lion for Lewis
   Jake and Honeybunch Go to Heaven
   Pig Pig Rides
6. Mark and attach the large envelope to the bulletin board. Place the spoons in this envelope.

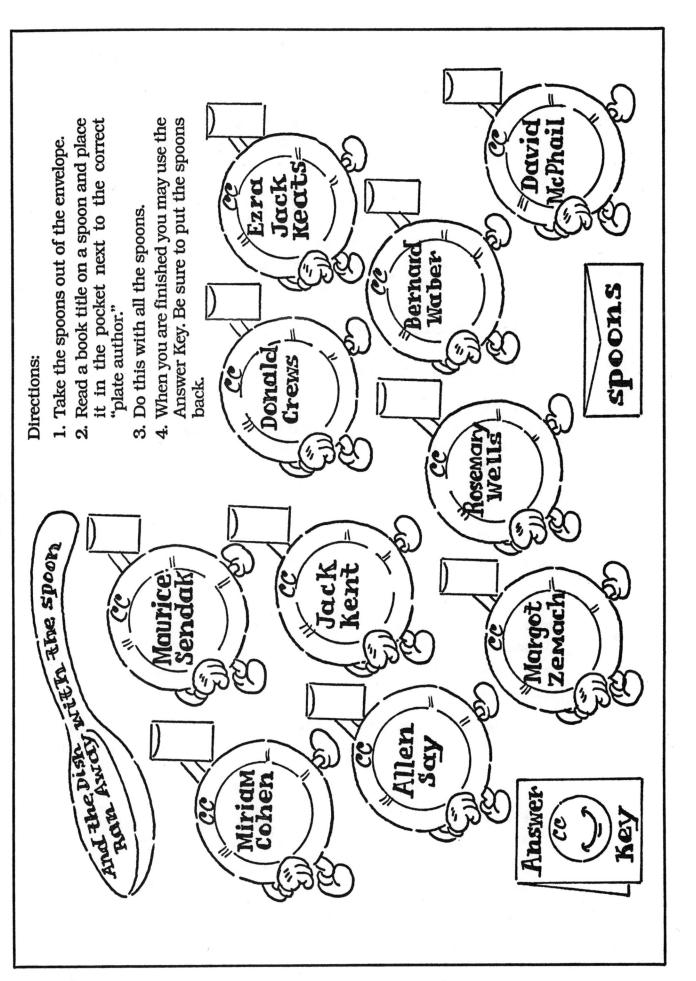

Directions:

1. Take the spoons out of the envelope.
2. Read a book title on a spoon and place it in the pocket next to the correct "plate author."
3. Do this with all the spoons.
4. When you are finished you may use the Answer Key. Be sure to put the spoons back.

And the Dish with the spoon Ran Away

Maurice Sendak

Jack Kent

Ezra Jack Keats

Donald Crews

Bernard Waber

David McPhail

Rosemary Wells

Margot Zemach

Miriam Cohen

Allen Say

spoons

Answer Key

7. Fold the white construction paper and mark the cover "Answer Key" as shown in the illustration. Copy the following on the inside and attach to the board:

   So What? by Miriam Cohen

   The Sign on Rosie's Door by Maurice Sendak

   Carousel by Donald Crews

   Peter's Chair by Ezra Jack Keats

   The Caterpillar and the Polliwog by Jack Kent

   The Bicycle Man by Allen Say

   Bernard by Bernard Waber

   A Lion for Lewis by Rosemary Wells

   Jake and Honeybunch Go to Heaven by Margot Zemach

   Pig Pig Rides by David McPhail

Bulletin Board Use:

Children are to place the spoons in the correct pockets by matching the book titles on the spoons with the authors' names on the plates. They may use the Answer Key when finished.

SUPER SCHOOL STORIES

Materials Needed:

large cardboard box

latex paint

razor-blade knife

tape

pillows

school storybooks

Construction Directions:

1. Cut and mark the large cardboard box using the schoolhouse pattern.

2. Fold back the sides of the box and use masking tape to attach the sides to the wall.

   NOTE: Be sure to draw or paint the windows. Do not cut them out because this will weaken the structure of the box.

3. Place the pillows and schoolbooks inside the school house display. You may want to use some of the following books in your display:

   I'd Rather Stay Home by Carol Barkin

   Miss Nelson Is Back by Harry Allard

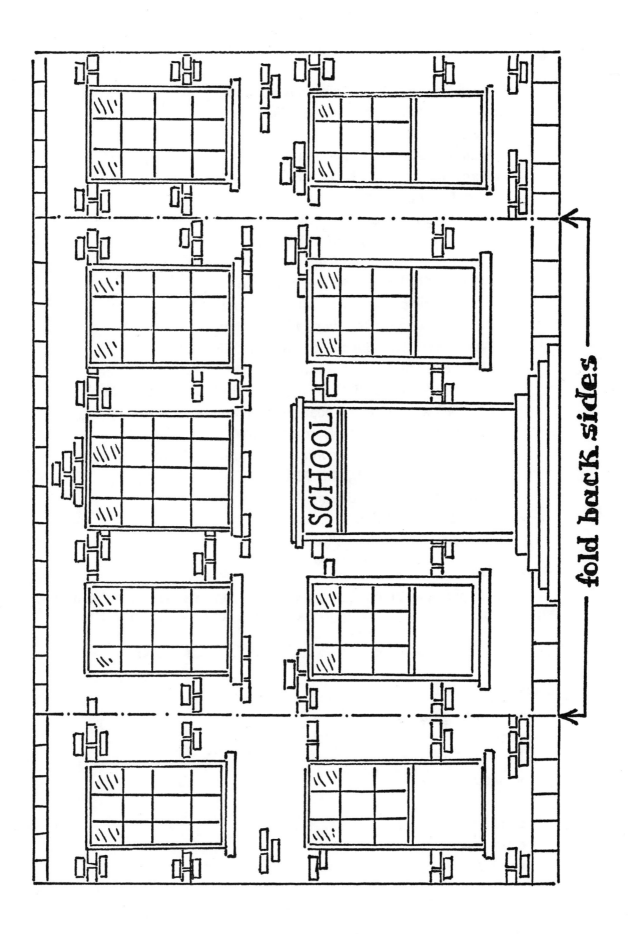

SCHOOL

fold back sides

Miss Nelson Is Missing by Harry Allard
The Very Worst Thing by Berthe Amoss
Ellen Tebbits by Beverly Cleary
Ramona the Pest by Beverly Cleary
Ramona the Brave by Beverly Cleary
Best Friends by Miriam Cohen
First Grade Takes a Test by Miriam Cohen
No Good in Art by Miriam Cohen
Tough Jim by Miriam Cohen
When Will I Read? by Miriam Cohen
Will I Have a Friend? by Miriam Cohen
Ethan's Favorite Teacher by Hila Colman
Next Year I'll Be Special by Patricia Reilly Giff
Willy Bear by Mildred Kantrowitz
The Day Jimmy's Boa Ate the Wash by Trinka Hakes Noble
Mrs. Peloki's Snake by Joanne Oppenheim
The Balancing Girl by Berniece Rabe
Thomas James the Second and Friends by Dorothy Richards
Jill Wins a Friend by Kay Rivers
My School by Peter Spier
How I Faded Away by Janice Udry
Hickory Stick Rag by Clyde Watson

Display Use:

This display may be used to interest children in stories about school. Be sure to limit the number of children using the center at any one time.

READING IS A LIFE PRESERVER!

Materials Needed:

white background paper
construction paper (various colors)
felt-tipped pens (various colors)
scissors
ditto box
ditto master
ditto paper
stapler

Construction Directions:

1. Use an opaque projector to trace the lettering and figures onto the background paper.
2. Cut life preservers out of the construction paper using an enlargement of the pattern shown here.

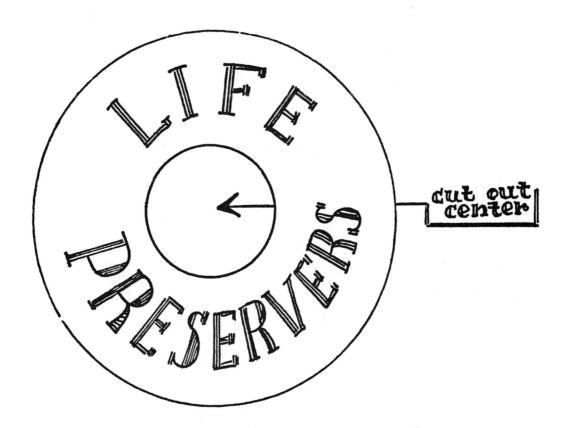

3. Attach the life preservers to the board by stapling only the top. This way they can be lifted from the bottom in order to insert the children's drawings.
4. Cut the ditto box in half across the width, cover with construction paper, print "Life Preservers" on the front, and attach it to the board.
5. Make copies of the "Life Preserver" sheets and place a supply in the bulletin board box.

Bulletin Board Use:

The children are to take a "Life Preserver Sheet" and draw one of their favorite parts in the circle. When finished, they are to return the sheet so you may display it on the bulletin board.

READING IS A LIFE PRESERVER!

Directions:

1. Take a life preserver sheet.
2. Read a book and draw a picture of one of the parts you liked best.
3. Give it to your teacher.
4. Look for it on this board!

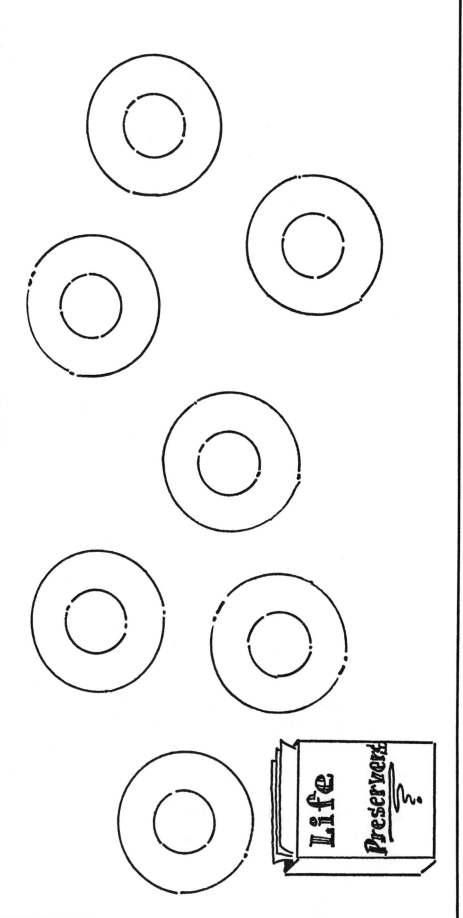

LIFE PRESERVER SHEET

In the circle, draw a picture of your favorite part of a book you just read. When you finish, give it to your teacher. It may be a real life preserver!

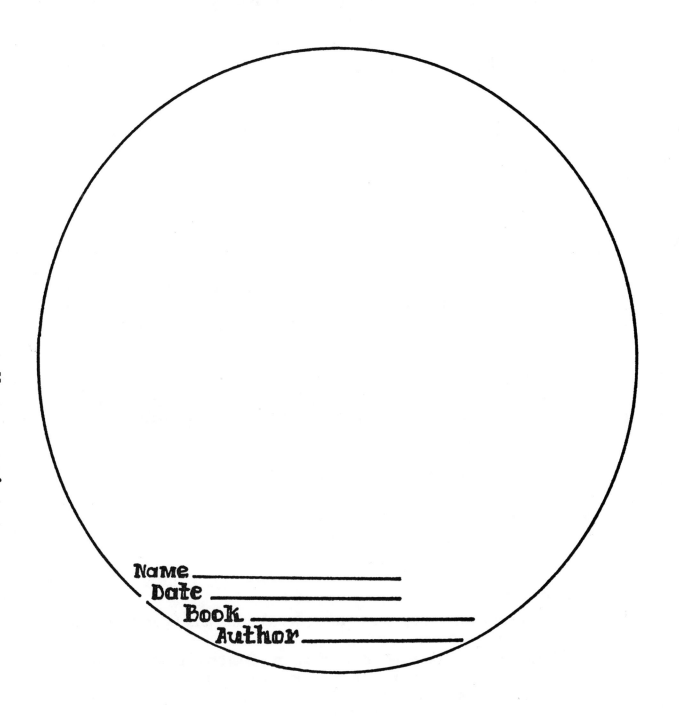

Name _____
Date _____
Book _____
Author _____

GOING BANANAS OVER READING

Materials Needed:

white background paper
felt-tipped pens (various colors)
ditto box
ditto master
yellow ditto paper
scissors
stapler

Construction Directions:

1. Use an opaque projector to trace the lettering and figures onto the background paper. Use appropriate colors for the tree and monkey.
2. Cut the ditto box in half across the width, cover with yellow paper, print "Banana Sheets" on the front, and attach it to the board.
3. Make copies of the "Going Bananas" sheets and place a supply in the bulletin board box.

Bulletin Board Use:

After reading a book, the children take one of the "Going Bananas" sheets and fill it in. When finished, they are to cut out the banana and return it to you so you may display it on the bulletin board. Watch the tree sprout bananas!

BOOKS YOU CAN'T *BEAR* TO PUT DOWN!

Materials Needed:

white background paper
felt-tipped pens (various colors)

Construction Directions:

1. Use an opaque projector to trace the lettering and figures onto the background paper.
2. Choose from the following list of books, titles, and authors to copy in the bear's footprints. Be sure the ones you choose are available in your classroom or school library:

   Winnie the Pooh by A.A. Milne

   Deep in the Forest by Brinton Turkle

   The Bear's Toothache by David McPhail

GOING BANANAS OVER READING

Read a book and then fill in the banana.
Cut it out and give it to your teacher.
Congratulations . . . you are helping the
tree sprout new bananas.

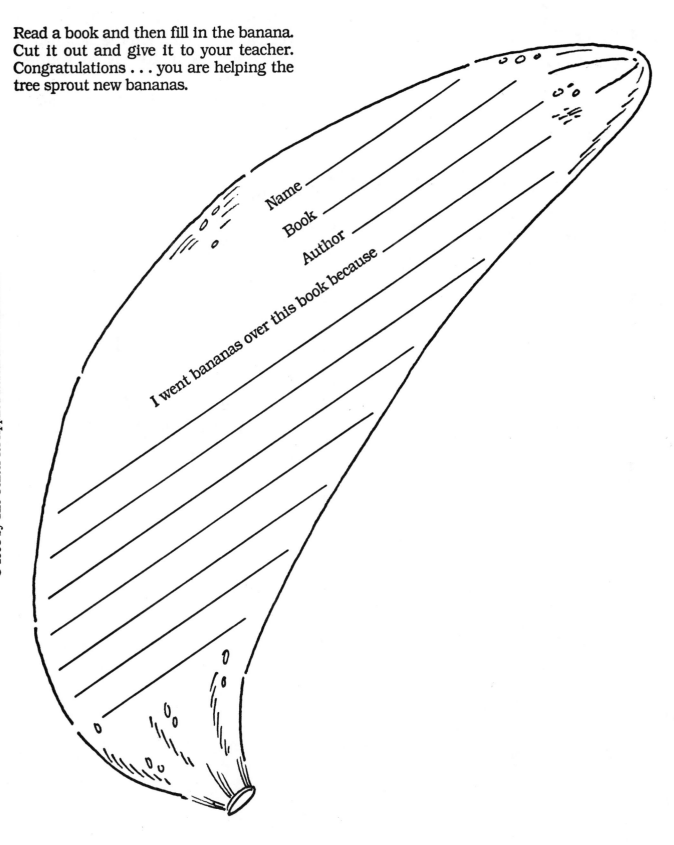

Name _____

Book _____

Author _____

I went bananas over this book because

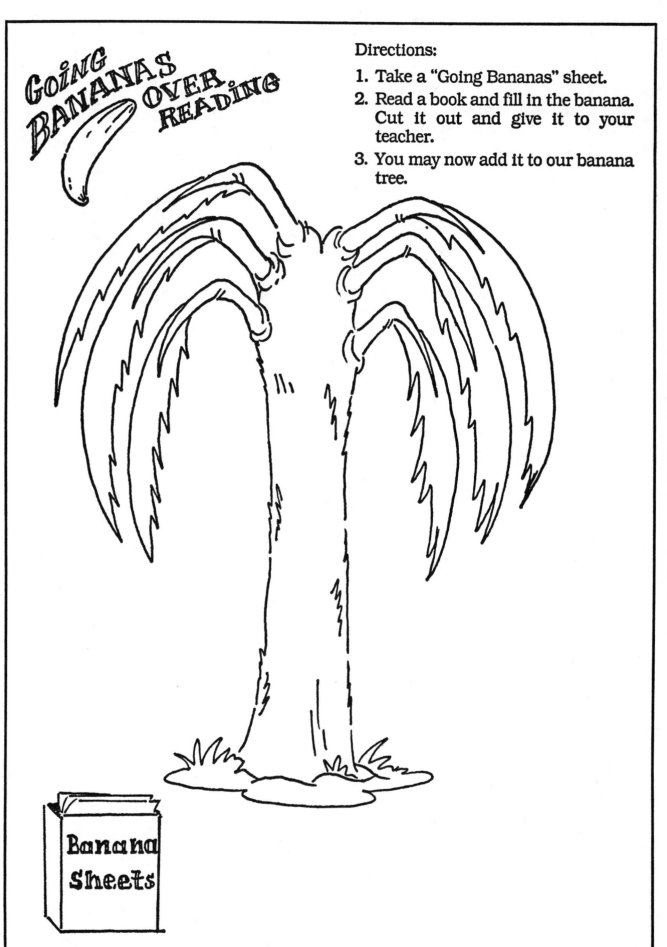

Going Bananas Over Reading

Directions:

1. Take a "Going Bananas" sheet.
2. Read a book and fill in the banana. Cut it out and give it to your teacher.
3. You may now add it to our banana tree.

Banana Sheets

BOOKS YOU CAN'T

BEAR

TO PUT DOWN !!

You'll find it unBEARable
not to read one of these!

The Biggest Bear by Lynd Ward

Blueberries for Sal by Robert McCloskey

Corduroy by Don Freeman

Henry Bear's Park by David McPhail

Little Bear by Else Minarik

Nobody Listens to Andrew by Elizabeth Guilfoile

The Three Bears by Paul Galdone

Moon Bear by Frank Asch

Panda by Susan Bonners

Little Koala by Tony Chen

Big Bear by Jean-Claude Brisville

Bear Hunt by Anthony Browne

A Pocket for Corduroy by Don Freeman

Panda's Puzzle and His Voyage of Discovery by Michael Foreman

The House of Five Bears by Cynthia Jameson

Mumble Bear by Gina Ruck-Panquet

Big Bad Bruce by Bill Peet

Bear's Bicycle by David McPhail

A Bear Called Paddington by Michael Bond

Bear Party by William Pene du Bois

More About Paddington by Michael Bond

Bear Circus by William Pene du Bois

Bulletin Board Use:

This bulletin board may be used to stimulate children's interest in books about bears.

BOOKS FOR A RAINY DAY

Materials Needed:

white background paper

felt-tipped pens (various colors)

blue construction paper

scissors

small gelatin or pudding boxes

stapler

glue

long thumbtacks

small umbrella

child's rain gear (coat, hat, boots)

Construction Directions:

1. Use an opaque projector to trace the lettering and storm clouds onto the background paper.
2. Attach the rain gear using the long thumbtacks.
3. Cut the raindrops out of the blue construction paper using an enlargement of the pattern shown here.

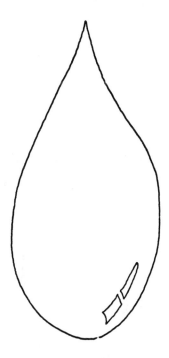

4. Copy the following, each on a different raindrop:
   Peter Spier's Rain by Peter Spier
   Rain by Robert Kalon
   Where Does the Butterfly Go When It Rains by May Garelick
   Annie's Rainbow by Ron Brooks
   Caught in the Rain by Beatrix Ferro
   Rain Makes Applesauce by Julian Scheer
   Aio, The Rainmaker by Fiona French
5. Attach the raindrops to the board with the small gelatin boxes as backing for a three-dimensional effect. Staple the boxes to the board and then glue the rain drops to these boxes.

Bulletin Board Use:

This bulletin board may be used to stimulate children's interest in books with *rain* in their titles.

Books for A RAINY DAY!

Don't be all wet!
Read one of these books.

READING IS TERRIF<u>EGG</u>!

Materials Needed:

> white background paper
> felt-tipped pens (various colors)

Construction Directions:

1. Use an opaque projector to trace the lettering and figures onto the background paper.
2. Copy the following, each on a different egg:
   Chickens Aren't the Only Ones by Ruth Heller
   Mushy Eggs by Florence Adams
   The Egg Book by Jack Kent
   Green Eggs and Ham by Dr. Seuss
   Horton Hatches the Egg by Dr. Seuss
   The Egg Tree by Katherine Milhous

Bulletin Board Use:

The bulletin board may be used to stimulate children's interest in books having the word *egg* in their titles.

READING IS TERRIFEGG!

Here are some
EGGsamples of
good reading!

Books can make you
EGGstatic! Read some
of these.

Skills Builders

Classification/Relationships
Sight Word Knowledge
Initial Consonants
Final Consonants
Medial Vowels
Consonant Blends
Contractions
Compound Words
Synonyms and Antonyms
Context Clue Usage
Main Ideas
Important Details
Sequence of Events

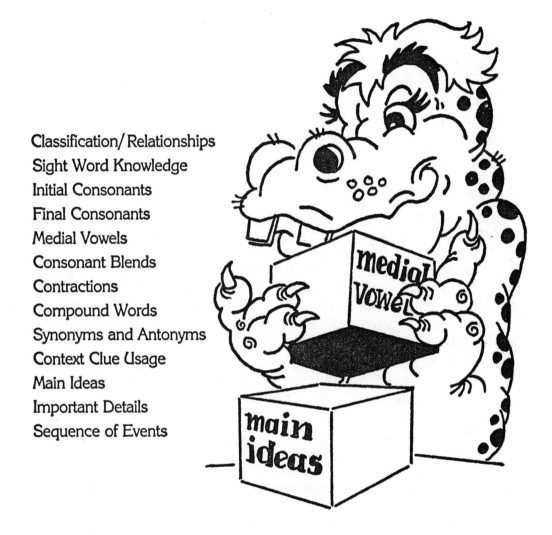

    While bulletin boards and displays help to create an attractive classroom, this does not have to be their only function. You can construct bulletin boards and displays that will help you reinforce the reading skills you are currently teaching.

    This section presents fifty-two different bulletin boards and displays that reinforce reading skills. These are organized into thirteen different skill areas each containing an introductory teaching lesson. Each bulletin board and display includes a list of simple materials needed for its construction. The size of the materials will depend on your available space. You will also find easy-to-follow directions for constructing each display and instructions for using the board to reinforce a specific reading skill.

CLASSIFICATION/RELATIONSHIPS

Introductory Lesson

Objective:

Children will be able to classify objects according to stated categories.

Materials Needed:

library books   ditto paper
chalkboard   30 sheets of 6" x 8" posterboard
ditto master

Introduction

Have a stack of books sitting on the edge of your desk or table in front of the children. As you begin your lesson, reach for something on your desk and "accidentally" knock the books onto the floor.

Explain to the children that you had placed the books in order according to two categories. Write "Animals" and "Plants" on the chalkboard. As a volunteer helps to pick up the books, ask the children to suggest in which stack (animal or plant) to place them. Before deciding, you will have to read the title and show the cover illustration.

> IMPORTANT: You will need to have collected a stack of books half of which are about animals (see 591 of nonfiction) and half concerning plants (see 574 of nonfiction).

Procedure:

Explain to the children that they are now going to take a "listening walk" around the school. They are to listen and remember as many sounds as they can along the way. After returning from the walk, ask the class to tell you the sounds they heard as you write them on the chalkboard.

> NOTE: Children may give you a few "imaginary" sounds. This is fine as they may still be used in the lesson.

Once you have exhausted the "sound ideas," tell the children that they are now to place all these sounds into one of several categories. Copy the following categories on the chalkboard:

PEOPLE   ANIMALS   MACHINES   NATURE

Now proceed down the list of sounds asking volunteers to place them under the appropriate heading. Make sure the children understand why each sound is being placed in that particular category.

Explain to the students they are now going to play the "Guess the Category Game" in order to practice their classification skills. You will need to copy each of the following drawings on a different 6" x 8" posterboard piece before the game. (Use an opaque projector.) Each player will need a card.

Copy the following on the chalkboard:

ANIMALS   MACHINES   NATURE

Now divide the children into two teams and pass out one card to every child and explain that you will point to one of the categories on the chalkboard list. If they think that the picture card fits in that category they should hold it up. If not, they keep it on their laps.

NOTE: Be sure they have just a few seconds in which to decide.

Each team should receive a point for each *correct* response. After this is done and marked on the board, all players exchange cards and you point to another category. The game continues in this manner until one team reaches 100. This team is the winner.

Evaluation:

Use the activity sheet "Sky or Land?" to see how well your children understand classification skills.

Before distributing copies of the activity sheet, you should copy the following scene on the chalkboard or a transparency.

Name _____

Date _____

Some things belong on the land and other things belong in the sky. Cut out the word squares below and paste them where they belong.

house	tree	bird	sun	airplane	car	moon	tent
cat	kite	worm	cloud	street	dog	star	train

Ask several volunteers to draw something they would expect to find in the sky or on the land. They should draw them in the appropriate places on the board. When you think your students understand the procedures, distribute the activity sheet and let them begin. You should take note of those students having difficulty with this assignment and plan a special group session to reteach them classification.

The activity sheet is easily corrected. Simply see that the following items have been pasted accordingly:

SKY	LAND
kite	house
bird	cat
sun	tree
cloud	worm
airplane	street
moon	car
star	dog
	tent
	train

Bulletin Boards & Displays for Skill Reinforcement

The following bulletin boards and displays have been designed to provide the children with meaningful practice in classification skills.

Display Number One: Sylvia the Sea Monster

Materials Needed:

blue background paper

felt-tipped pens (various colors)

straight pins

white posterboard

scissors

stapler

hole punch

blue construction paper

legal-size envelope

Construction Directions:

1. Use an opaque projector to trace the lettering and figures in the bulletin board illustration onto the background paper.

2. Place the straight pins on the board as shown.

3. Cut and mark the white posterboard using the shell pattern.

4. Print each of the following words on a different shell as shown in the illustration:

drum	shoe
banana	cap
dog	fork
bat	glass
boat	table

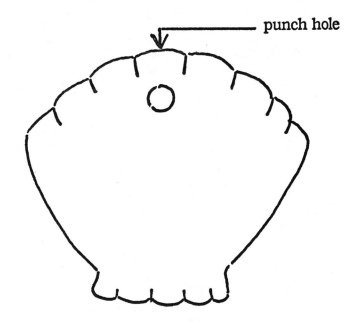

punch hole

5. Attach the large envelope to the board and place the shells in it.

6. Fold a sheet of construction paper and mark "Answer Key" on the cover. Copy the following inside and attach to the board:

horn – drum	sock – shoe
apple – banana	hat – cap
cat – dog	spoon – fork
ball – bat	cup – glass
car – boat	chair – table

Bulletin Board Use:

The children are to hang the shells on the appropriate hooks according to their category. When finished, they are to check the Answer Key.

SYLVIA THE SEA MONSTER

Directions:

1. Take the shells out of the envelope.
2. Follow Sylvia's path. Each time you come to a fish, look through the shells to find an object that has something in common with the object in that fish.
3. Hang the shells on the hooks as you do this.
4. When you finish, use the Answer Key.

Display Number Two: Pick a Pocket

Materials Needed:

background paper
apron with two pockets
felt-tipped pens (various colors)
posterboard
scissors
construction paper
stapler
thumbtacks
legal-size envelope

Construction Directions:

1. Use an opaque projector to trace the lettering onto the background paper as shown in the bulletin board illustration.
2. Attach the apron and print "clothes" on one pocket and "food" on the other.
3. Cut and mark the posterboard using an enlargement of the mitten pattern shown here. You will need ten.

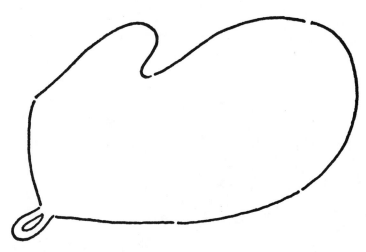

4. Copy the following, each on a different mitten:

hat	pie
shoes	cake
shirt	hamburger
belt	corn
dress	potatoes

Pick A Pocket

food

clothes

Directions:

1. Take the mittens out of the envelope.
2. Look at one of the mittens. In which pocket should it be placed? Put it in the right pocket.
3. Do this with all the mittens.
4. When finished, you may look in the Answer Key.

mittens

Answer Key

5. Attach the large envelope to the board and place the mittens in it.

6. Fold a sheet of construction paper and mark "Answer Key" on the cover. Now copy the following on the inside and attach it to the board:

CLOTHES	FOOD
hat	pie
shoes	cake
shirt	hamburger
belt	corn
dress	potatoes

Bulletin Board Use:

The children are to place the mittens into the appropriate pockets according to their category. When finished, they are to check the Answer Key.

Display Number Three: Hang It Up!

Materials Needed:

shoe box	felt-tipped pen
two coat hangers	16 paper clips
construction paper	posterboard
scissors	hole punch
tape	

Construction Directions:

1. Copy the words "Plants" and "Animals" on construction paper and tape them to the coat hangers as shown here.

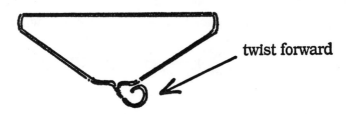

twist forward

2. Use an opaque projector to trace the following lettering and figures onto a sheet of construction paper.

Directions:

1. Take a card from the box.
2. Is it plant or animal?
3. Hang it on the correct hook.
4. Look at the Answer Key when you finish.

3. Fold a sheet of construction paper and mark the cover "Answer Key." Copy the following on the inside:

Animal	Plant
dog	bean
cat	rose
mouse	grass
cow	flower
horse	weed
sheep	lily
pig	carrot
hen	lettuce

4. Attach the hangers, directions, and answer key to a wall in an "out-of-the-way" place in your classroom. They should be low enough so a child may sit on the floor and use the display.

5. Cover the box with construction paper and print "Hang It Up!" on the front. Place this box under the hangers.

6. Cut and punch the posterboard as shown here. You will need 16 circles.

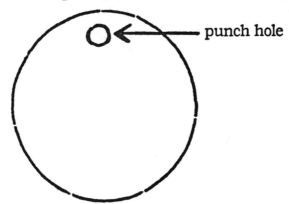

punch hole

7. Print the following, each on a different circle, and place in the box:

dog, cat, mouse, cow, horse, sheep, pig, hen
bean, rose, grass, flower, weed, lily, carrot, lettuce

Display Use:

The children hang the circle tags on the correct hook: either animal or plant. When they finish, they may use the Answer Key.

Display Number Four: Inside or Outside

Materials Needed:

white background paper
felt-tipped pens (various colors)
two shoe box lids
thumbtacks
construction paper
stapler
scissors
tape
shoelaces

Construction Directions:

1. Use an opaque projector to trace the lettering and figures onto the background paper.
2. Cover the box lids, punch three holes in each, and attach to the board.
3. Attach a shoelace on each picture using a thumbtack.
4. Fold a sheet of construction paper and mark "Answer Key" on the cover. Copy the following on the inside and staple it to the board:

Inside	Outside
bed	tree
TV	swing
lamp	car

Bulletin Board Use:

The children thread the shoelaces into the correct box: either inside or outside. When they finish, they may use the Answer Key.

Directions:

1. Look at a picture. Would you find it inside or outside?

2. When you know, put the shoelace in that box.

3. Look at the Answer Key when you are done.

BOX

OUTSIDE

INSIDE

Answer Key

BOX

SIGHT WORD KNOWLEDGE

Introductory Lesson

Objective:

Students will be able to recognize selected whole words by sight.

Materials Needed:

chalkboard
construction paper
tape

Introduction

Copy the following on the chalkboard.

Print the following words, each on a different sheet of construction paper. Be sure to circle the letter that is circled in each word:

gho(s)t, n(o)se, l(a)mp, t(e)nt, fi(s)h, eig(h)t, t(e)n, (r)ain

Explain to the children that they are to place the word cards over the pictures on the board. Place the word cards on the chalk tray and have volunteers tape them to the board. When finished, explain that if they were correct, the circled letters will spell where the family in the car is going. (See the Answer Key.) Ask for students to copy the circled letters, in order, on the chalkboard spaces.

```
ANSWER KEY
S    fi(s)h
E    t(e)n
A    l(a)mp
S    gho(s)t
H    eig(h)t
O    n(o)se
R    (r)ain
E    t(e)nt
```

Procedure:

Explain to the children they are now going to play "Pantomime-a-Word Game." First copy the following words onto the chalkboard:

WALK   SKIP   JUMP   TURN
CREEP   RUN   HOP   SIT

Now have volunteers come to the front of the class and pantomime one of the words. When each "actor" is finished, have other students guess the word by walking to the chalkboard and pointing to it.

Once all these words have been pantomimed, copy the next group of more difficult words on the board and continue the activity:

THIS   CLOUDY   HORSE   ROCKET
TAKE   LIKE   ELEPHANT   HORRIBLE

SUGGESTION: The children would love to have you participate in this activity. Perhaps you could be the first to pantomime so everyone understands what they are to do.

Evaluation:

Use the activity sheet "Go Fly a Kite" to see how well your students recognize sight words.

Before distributing copies of the activity sheet, you should copy the following on the chalkboard or a transparency:

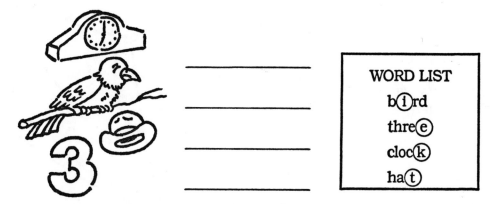

WORD LIST
b(i)rd
thre(e)
cloc(k)
ha(t)

Using the students' suggestions, fill in the words on the spaces next to their appropriate drawings. Be sure to circle the letters that are circled in the word list. Point out that these letters will spell something if they are correct. (See the Answer Key.) When you think your students understand the procedure, distribute the activity sheet and let them begin. You should take note of those children having difficulty with this assignment and plan a special group session to reteach selected sight words.

ANSWER KEY
K cloc(k)
I b(i)rd
T ha(t)
E thre(e)

The activity sheet is self-correcting. As shown in the Answer Key, the words ONE HUNDRED will be spelled if the sheet is completed correctly.

ANSWER KEY

O sciss(o)rs   H eig(h)t
N wi(n)dow   U fo(u)r
E peopl(e)   N mountai(n)
                     D (d)oor
                     R squa(r)e
                     E hous(e)
                     D nee(d)le

Name _____

Date _____

You're going to fly a kite today. First cut out the Word Boxes. Then look at the pictures on the kite string and match each word to its picture. Paste the Word Box on the correct picture. When you finish, begin with the first box by the hand and copy the circled letters on the spaces at the bottom of this page. If you are correct, these letters will spell how many feet in the sky you flew the kite.

WORD BOXES

nee(d)le
fo(u)r
wi(n)dow
mountai(n)
peopl(e)
eig(h)t
hous(e)
sciss(o)rs
squa(r)e
(d)oor

_ _ _ _

_ _ _ _ _ _ _ _ _

© 1998 by The Center for Applied Research in Education

Bulletin Boards & Displays for Skill Reinforcement

The following bulletin boards and displays have been designed to provide the children with meaningful practice in recognizing selected sight words.

Display Number One: Let's Play Badminton

Materials Needed:

background paper
badminton racket
long thumbtacks
felt-tipped pens (various colors)
construction paper
posterboard
legal-size envelope
straight pins
hole punch
scissors
stapler

Construction Directions:

1. Use an opaque projector to trace the figures and lettering onto the background paper.
2. Use the long thumbtacks to attach the badminton racket to the board.
3. Attach the straight pins as shown in the illustration.
4. Cut and mark the posterboard using an enlargement of the shuttlecock pattern.
5. Print each of the following words on a different shuttlecock as shown in the shuttlecock illustration:
   island, eight, knife, laugh, window, comb, phone
6. Mark "shuttlecocks" on the envelope, attach to the board, and place the shuttlecocks in it.
7. Fold a sheet of construction paper and mark "Answer Key" on the cover. Print the following on the inside and attach it to the board:

   1. island   5. knife
   2. window   6. phone
   3. eight   7. laugh
   4. comb

(hang real racket)

Directions:

1. Take the shuttlecocks out of the envelope.
2. Look at the word on one of the shuttlecocks. Find the drawing of that word on a racket. Hang the shuttlecock on that racket. Continue doing the same with the rest of the shuttlecocks.
3. Use the Answer Key when you finish.

shuttlecocks

1.

2.

3.

4.

5.

6.

7.

Answer Key

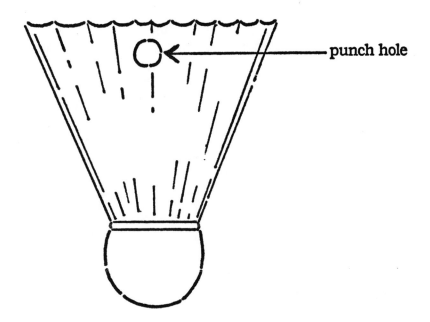

punch hole

Bulletin Board Use:

The children take the shuttlecocks out of the envelope. They are to match the words on the shuttlecocks with the drawings on the rackets. They do this by hanging the shuttlecocks on the rackets. They may use the Answer Key when they are finished.

Display Number Two: Pick a Pair

Materials Needed:

background paper
yellow construction paper
green construction paper
straight pins
2 legal-size envelopes
stapler
felt-tipped pen
scissors
construction paper

Construction Directions:

1. Use an opaque projector to trace the tree and lettering onto the background paper.
2. Stick the straight pins in the tree as shown in the illustration.

3. Cut the yellow and green construction paper pieces into pear shapes using an enlargement of the pattern shown here.

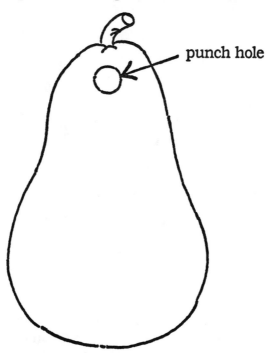

punch hole

4. Print each of the following words on a yellow pear:

   tale, knew, write, see, scent, break, bear, I, hour, threw, made, night, week, one, rain, dear, ate, feet

5. Print each of the following words on a green pear:

   tail, new, right, sea, sent, brake, bare, eye, our, through, maid, knight, weak, won, reign, deer, eight, feat

6. Attach the two envelopes to the bulletin board and print "Green Pears" on one and "Yellow Pears" on the other. Now put the pears into the appropriate envelopes.

7. Fold a sheet of construction paper and mark "Answer Key" on the cover. Copy the following on the inside and attach to the board:

tale – tail	threw – through
knew – new	made – maid
write – right	night – knight
see – sea	week – weak
scent – sent	one – won
break – brake	rain – reign
bear – bare	dear – deer
I – eye	ate – eight
hour – our	feet – feat

PICK A PAIR

Directions:

1. Take the pears out of the envelopes.
2. Look at one of the green pears. Can you find its homonym on one of the yellow pears? When you do hang them on one of the hooks.
3. Do the same with all the pears.
4. Use the Answer Key when you finish.

green pears

yellow pears

Answer Key

Bulletin Board Use:

The children take the pears out of the envelopes and try to find the matching homonyms. When they find a matching pair (one green and one yellow) they may hang them on the tree with one of the pins. When finished, they may use the Answer Key.

Display Number Three: Wagon of Words

Materials Needed:

small wagon	scissors
index cards	tape
felt-tipped pens (various colors)	construction paper
posterboard	small items to place in wagon

Construction Directions:

1. Cut and mark the posterboard using an enlargement of the wagon pattern shown here. Tape it to the wall just above the real wagon.

Directions:

1. Look at one of the word cards.
   Can you find the item in the wagon?
   When you do, place the item on that
   word card.
2. Continue to match the other word
   cards and items.
3. You may use the Answer Key when you
   finish.

2. Print the following words, each on a different index card and place a small (toy) example of each in the wagon.

   NOTE: Make up your own list according to the items you have readily available.

ball	cup
top	saucer
iron	plate
key	chalk
doll	block
spoon	train
fork	stone
knife	twig

3. Fold a sheet of construction paper and mark "Answer Key" on the cover. Copy the following on the inside and attach to the posterboard as shown in the illustration.

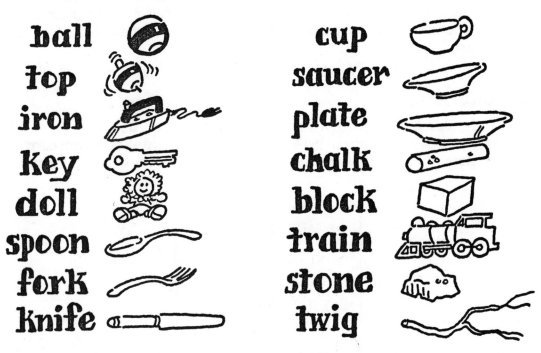

   NOTE: If you use different objects you will need to make small drawings of those.

Display Use:

The children are to match the objects in the wagon with the word cards. They do this by placing the objects on the appropriate word cards. They may use the Answer Key when they finish.

Display Number Four: Wordopolis

Materials Needed:

background paper
felt-tipped pens (various colors)
ditto box
ditto master
ditto paper
stapler
tape
scissors

Construction Directions:

1. Use an opaque projector to trace the lettering and figures onto the background paper.
2. Cut the ditto box in half across the width, cover with construction paper, print "Wordopolis Sheets" on the front, and attach it to the board.
3. Put copies of the "Wordopolis" sheet in the bulletin board box.

Bulletin Board Use:

The children take an activity sheet and match the words to their pictures. They are to copy down the circled letters from these words. If they are correct, these letters will spell the name of the Mayor of Wordopolis. (See the Answer Key.)

```
┌─────────────────────────┐
│        ANSWER KEY        │
│                          │
│    N    te(n)            │
│                          │
│    A    st(a)r           │
│                          │
│    T    (t)hree          │
│                          │
│    H    feat(h)er        │
│                          │
│    A    c(a)t            │
│                          │
│    N    rai(n)           │
│                          │
│    N    light(n)ing      │
│                          │
│    O    gh(o)st          │
│                          │
│    U    ho(u)s           │
│                          │
│    N    moo(n)           │
└─────────────────────────┘
```

WELCOME TO WORDOPOLIS

Can you guess who is the mayor of Wordopolis? Well, work a "Wordopolis Sheet" and find out!

Wordopolis Sheets

Name _____

Date _____

WORDOPOLIS SHEET

Find out the name of the mayor of Wordopolis.
All you have to do is work the puzzle on this
sheet. Look at the words in the Word List
below. You are to write the correct word next
to each drawing. Circle the same letter in each
word that is circled in the Word List. If you are
correct, the circled letters will spell the name
of the mayor.

_____

_____

_____

_____

_____

_____

_____

_____

```
┌─────────────────────────┐
│       WORD LIST         │
│   light(n)ing           │
│   st(a)r                │
│   feat(h)er             │
│   gh(o)st               │
│   te(n)                 │
│   c(a)t                 │
│   moo(n)                │
│   ho(u)se               │
│   (t)hree               │
│   rai(n)                │
└─────────────────────────┘
```

INITIAL CONSONANTS

Introductory Lesson

Objective:

Students will be able to make the correct association between selected consonants and their sounds when given in the initial position.

Materials Needed:

chalkboard
34 sheets of 4″ x 6″ posterboard
ditto master
ditto paper

Introduction:

A stimulating way in which to emphasize initial consonants is to use words in jingles and songs. Teach your students to sing the familiar Campbell's Soup song using the following words:

/m/, /m/ .... milk
/m/, /m/ .... man
That's how M is sounded
Met, mug, mouse.

Try these words for practicing other consonants:

/c/, /c/ .... cat
/c/, /c/ .... can
That's how C is sounded
Cap, coat, cup.

/s/, /s/ .... song
/s/, /s/ .... sat
That's how S is sounded
Sit, sap, sun.

/b/, /b/ .... bug
/b/, /b/ .... boy
That's how B is sounded
Bat, bang, boom.

/d/, /d/ .... dog
/d/, /d/ .... dish
That's how D is sounded
Day, doll, dig.

/f/, /f/ .... fat
/f/, /f/ .... fun
That's how F is sounded
Fan, full, for.

/h/, /h/ .... hat
/h/, /h/ .... hand
That's how H is sounded
Hit, hold, hop.

/j/, /j/ . . . . jump	/r/, /r/ . . . . run
/j/, /j/ . . . . joy	/r/, /r/ . . . . ran
That's how J is sounded	That's how R is sounded
Job, junk, jar.	Rug, rat, red.
/t/, /t/ . . . . toy	/p/, /p/ . . . . pen
/t/, /t/ . . . . tool	/p/, /p/ . . . . pop
That's how T is sounded	That's how P is sounded
Tan, tar, tap.	Pay, pan, pot.

Prior to singing each verse be sure to write the letter (both upper and lower case) on the chalkboard. After several have been done this way, ask for volunteers to go to the chalkboard, point to one of the letters, say a word that begins with that sound and lead the class in its song.

Procedure:

Write on the chalkboard the names of several children in the classroom (or other common first names) that begin with the same letter. For example:

Bill	Mike	Danny	Connie
Betty	Maria	Debbie	Carl
Bob	Mat	Dick	Candy

Pronounce each name and then have the class pronounce each name. Point out the fact that each name begins with the same letter and that this letter represents the same sound in each word.

Explain to the students that they are now going to play the "Animal Game" in order to practice beginning letter sounds in words.

You will need to copy the following letter pairs, each on *two* 4″ x 6″ poster-board pieces before the game:

Bb, Cc, Dd, Ff, Gg, Hh, Jj, Ll,

Mm, Nn, Pp, Rr, Ss, Tt, Ww, Zz

Divide the class into two equal teams and pass out one card to each child. Do not pass out the same letter card to members of the same team. Now explain that you will read an animal name. If they are holding the letter card with which this name begins, they are to hold up the card. If not, they keep it on their lap.

Five points are given to each team every time their member correctly holds up a letter. If both teams correctly identify the same letter, they *both* receive five points.

NOTE: You should keep a running tally on the chalkboard of each team's score.

If more than one player on a team holds up their cards, no points are given, even if one of the cards contained the correct letter. The game continues until all the words on the "Animal Name List" have been read. The team with the most points is the winner.

ANIMAL NAME LIST	
fox	robin
dog	turtle
jackal	lizard
mouse	newt
bat	zebra
hen	pig
cat	horse
pigeon	salamander
cow	rabbit
lion	wolf
bear	bug
goat	worm
rooster	fish

Evaluation:

Use the activity sheet "Dog Gone!" to see how well your students understand initial consonant sound/letter relationships.

Before distributing copies of the activity sheet you should copy the following on the chalkboard or transparency:

Tt

Bb

Hh

Using the students' suggestions, draw a line from each object to its beginning consonant sound. (See the Answer Key.)

DOG GONE!

Name _____

Date _____

Match the bones and the dogs by drawing a line from each object in the bone to its beginning consonant sound on the dog.

```
ANSWER KEY
t – top
b – ball
h – heart
```

The activity sheet is easily corrected. Simply check to see that the drawings and letters have been matched as shown in the Answer Key.

```
ANSWER KEY
t – tent
c – can
p – pumpkin
g – ghost
s – sun
f – fish
```

Bulletin Boards/Displays for Skill Reinforcement

The following bulletin boards and displays have been designed to provide the students with meaningful practice in initial consonant recognition.

Display Number One: Pirate Pickworth's Pistol

Materials Needed:

white background paper
blue construction paper
gray posterboard
legal-size envelope
felt-tipped pens (various colors)
straight pins
scissors
paper hole punch
stapler
large feather

Construction Directions:

1. Use an opaque projector to trace the figures and lettering onto the background paper.
2. Place the straight pins on the board as shown in the illustration.
3. Attach the feather by using straight pins.
4. Cut the gray posterboard using the gunshot pattern shown here.

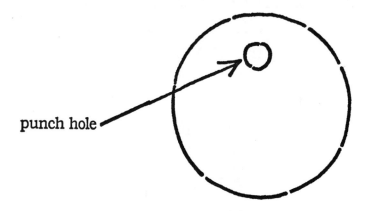

punch hole

5. Copy each of these letter pairs on a different shot:
   Tt, Mm, Hh, Ff, Ss, Nn, Ll, Cc, Bb, Pp
6. Attach the large envelope to the board and mark "shots" on it. Place the gunshots in it.
7. Fold the blue construction paper and mark the cover "Answer Key" as shown in the illustration. Copy the following on the inside and attach to the board:

t – ten	n – needle
m – moon	l – lightning
h – hat	c – cat
f – feather	b – box
s – sock	p – pen

Bulletin Board Use:

Children are to match the objects on the board with their beginning sounds on the gunshots by placing the shots on the appropriate pins. They may use the Answer Key when finished.

> NOTE: You should read the directions aloud to the class and then discuss the procedure prior to the students' using it.

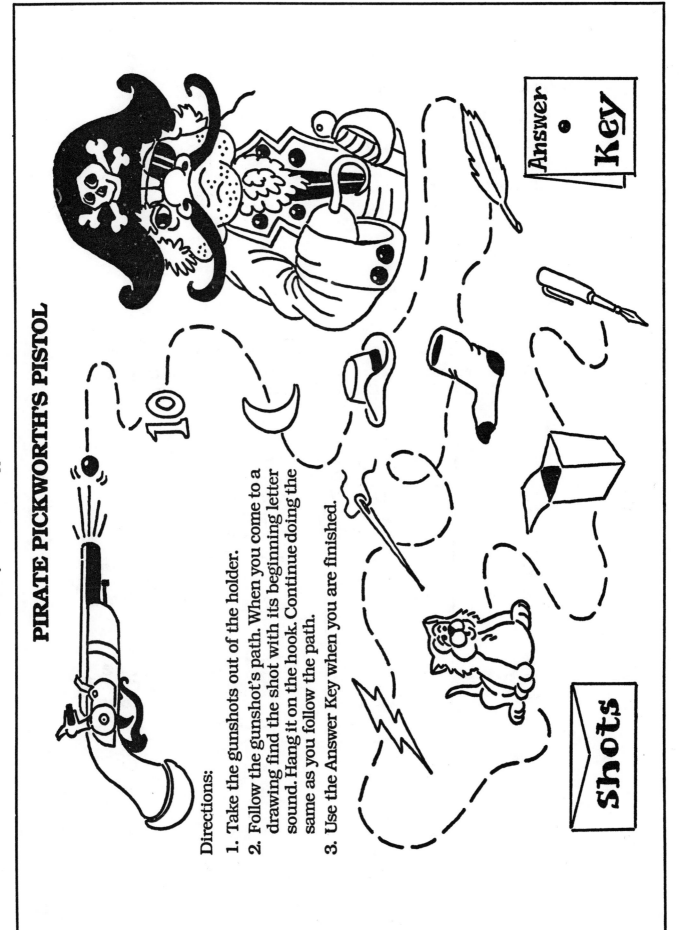

© 1998 by The Center for Applied Research in Education

PIRATE PICKWORTH'S PISTOL

Directions:

1. Take the gunshots out of the holder.
2. Follow the gunshot's path. When you come to a drawing find the shot with its beginning letter sound. Hang it on the hook. Continue doing the same as you follow the path.
3. Use the Answer Key when you are finished.

Shots

Answer • Key

Display Number Two: Consonant Curtains

Materials Needed:

> curtains and adjustable rod
> construction paper
> felt-tipped pens (various colors)
> magazine pictures
> magazine/catalog
> scissors
> glue
> pins

Construction Directions:

1. Hang the curtains in an appropriate location in your classroom.
2. Use the construction paper to trace and cut letters from the patterns to form the title. See the "Consonant Curtains" illustration.

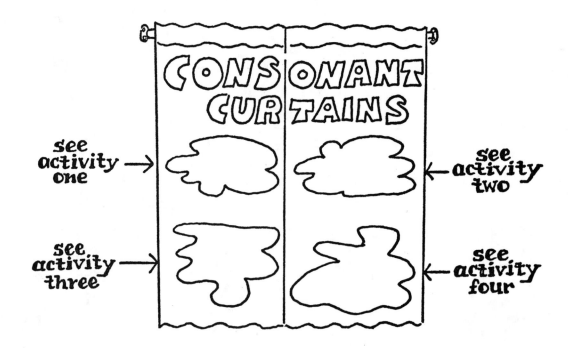

C O A

N

N R

S I

I R

T U

3. Use construction paper and magazine pictures, where indicated, to prepare the following activities and instructions for the students. Attach them to the curtain as shown in the illustration.

Activity One

picture of something beginning with "b" consonant

Find five pictures of things in a magazine that begin with the /b/ sound. Cut these out and paste them on a sheet of paper. Write the word of the object under each picture.

Activity Two

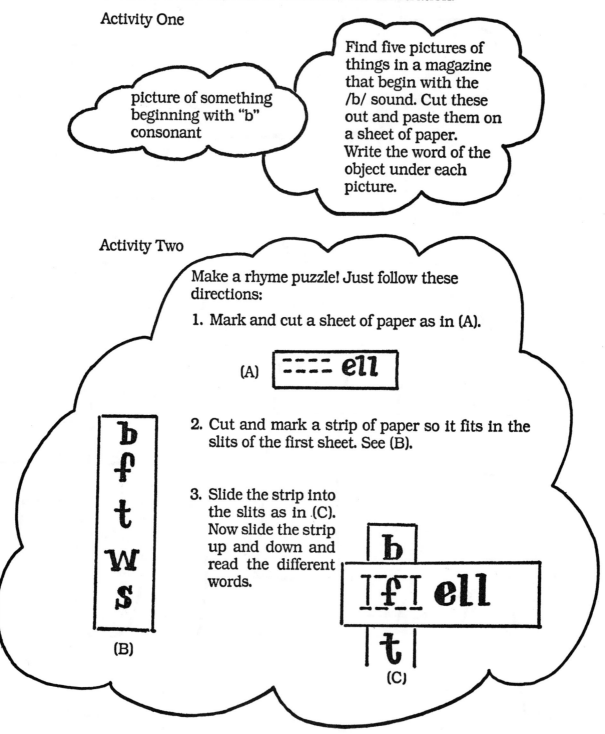

Make a rhyme puzzle! Just follow these directions:

1. Mark and cut a sheet of paper as in (A).

(A) ==== ell

2. Cut and mark a strip of paper so it fits in the slits of the first sheet. See (B).

3. Slide the strip into the slits as in (C). Now slide the strip up and down and read the different words.

b
f
t
w
s

(B)

b
f ell
t

(C)

Activity Three

How many words can you think of that begin with the letter "t"? Write them down. Here are a few pictures to help get you started.

pictures of objects beginning with "t"

Activity Four

Copy this paragraph and fill in the missing words. I've given you the first letter to help you get going!

Dad and I went to l_____ for a dog. We found a b_____ one at the pound. He is black with w_____ spots. We call him S_____.

Display Use:

Students are to work through the four activities on the curtain.

Display Number Three: Cheeta Swings

Materials Needed:

    white background paper
    tan posterboard
    green posterboard
    green construction paper
    felt-tipped pens (various colors)
    long thumbtacks
    small gelatin boxes
    glue
    scissors
    stapler

Construction Directions:

1. Use an opaque projector to trace, cut, and mark the tree trunk and tree leaves from the tan and green posterboard. Attach the small gelatin boxes to the board and glue the tree to these. This will give a three-dimensional effect.

2. Cut and mark the tan posterboard using the Cheeta pattern.

Directions:

1. Look at the first monkey. Say the sound of the letter on this monkey. Which object in the pictures next to the monkey begins with this sound? Swing the monkey toward that picture.

2. Keep on doing the same with each of the monkeys.

3. When you finish, use the Answer Key to find out how many times you were right!

Cheeta Swings

Answer Key

Hh

Ss

Ff

Tt

Bb

Cc

3. Copy each of the following letter pairs on a different monkey as shown in the illustration:

   Bb, Ff, Hh, Cc, Tt, Ss

4. Using the thumbtacks, attach these to the board as shown on the bulletin board illustration.

5. Use the opaque projector to finish tracing the figures and lettering as shown in the illustration.

6. Fold the green construction paper to form an Answer Key and mark the front cover as shown. Mark the following on the inside and attach to the board:

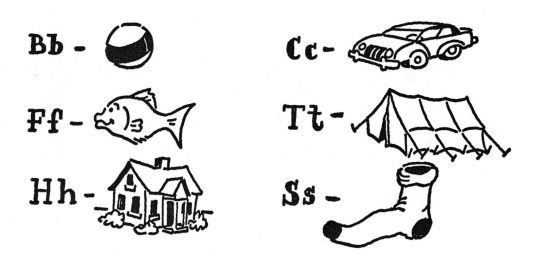

Bulletin Board Use:

Children look at the letter on the monkey and match this to the beginning sound of the objects in the drawings on either side. They do this by swinging the monkey toward the appropriate drawing. They may use the Answer Key when they are finished.

Display Number Four: Karl's Quiet Corner

Materials Needed:

heavyweight posterboard   scissors
lightweight posterboard   glue
felt-tipped pens (various colors)   small throw rug
a small basket   envelope
pincher clothespins

Construction Directions:

1. Mark and cut a large sheet of heavyweight posterboard using an enlargement of the pattern shown in the display.

2. Cut and attach a piece of heavy posterboard as shown here.

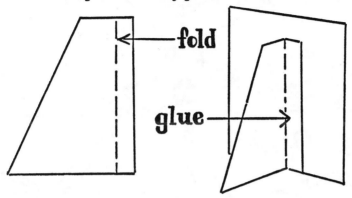

3. Mark the following letter pairs, each on a different clothespin:

    Cc, Pp, Rr, Bb, Ll, Ff, Tt, Ss, Hh, Gg, Ww, Dd

4. Put the clothespins in a basket on a small rug in front of the display.

5. Make an answer key by copying the following on a sheet of lightweight posterboard and placing it in an envelope. Mark "Answer Key" on the envelope and place it near the display.

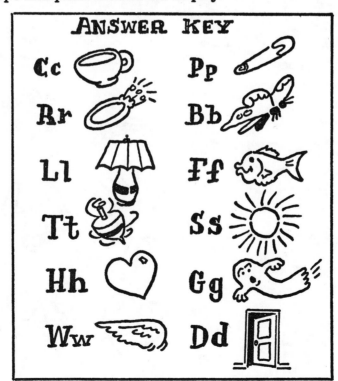

Display Use:

The children are to match the beginning sounds in the drawings with the letters on the clothespins. They do this by attaching the appropriate clothespin next to each drawing. Students may use the Answer Key when they finish.

FINAL CONSONANTS

Introductory Lesson

Objective:

Children will be able to make the correct association between selected consonants and their sounds when given in the final position.

Materials Needed:

ditto master	tape
ditto paper	chalkboard
scissors	transparency
construction paper	*The Cat in the Hat* by Dr. Seuss
paste	(Houghton Mifflin, 1957)

Introduction:

Make a transparency of the picture collage shown on the next page. You might make a thermal transparency on your school copier.

Copy the following letters on the chalkboard:

/D/ /G/ /T/ /L/ /N/ /K/ /S/

Now show the children the transparency. Tell the students that each "thing" in the collage ends with one of the consonant sounds on the chalkboard. Using the students' suggestions, copy the items under the appropriate letter sounds. (See the Answer Key.)

ANSWER KEY						
/D/	/G/	/T/	/L/	/N/	/K/	/S/
bird	dog	cat	ball	ten	hook	mouse
bed	bug	hat	bell	sun	sock	house
log	pig	bat	wall	pumpkin	duck	bus
sled	egg	heart	pill	can	truck	
		tent	well	phone	rake	

Procedure:

Tell the children you are going to read them the story, *The Cat in the Hat* by Dr. Seuss. They are going to have to be very good listeners because they will be expected to pay close attention to the ending word sounds. Each time they hear certain sounds they will be expected to do certain things. Copy the following on the chalkboard:

/T/   clap hands together once

/L/   raise one hand in the air

/N/   turn head to each side

SUGGESTION: Practice each of the actions by slowly reading the first page. They should respond to the following words: sun, not, it, wet, sat, in, all, that, and wet.

Once the children understand the directions, proceed with reading the story to its completion. You might want to add ending sounds along with appropriate reactions. For example, /P/, stand up and sit back down, or /D/, place hands on head.

Evaluation:

Use the activity sheet "Ride the Roller Coaster" to see how well your children understand final consonant letter/sound relationships.

Before distributing copies of the activity sheet, you should copy the following on 9″ x 12″ construction paper:

T   N   G

Copy the following box drawings on the chalkboard. Be sure the boxes measure 9″ x 12″.

After placing the sheet of construction paper on the chalk tray so all children can see them, have them name what is in the first box. Have them repeat it, this time listening for the ending sound. Ask a volunteer to go to the board and hold up the letter card that represents this ending sound. If he is correct, have him tape it over the appropriate box. Continue to do this with the other two boxes. When you think your children understand the procedure, pass out the activity sheet and have them complete it.

Ride the Roller Coaster

Cut out the picture boxes at the bottom
of the page. Now take a ride on the
roller coaster. When you come to a
letter box, find a picture that
ends with that sound and paste
it over the letter box.

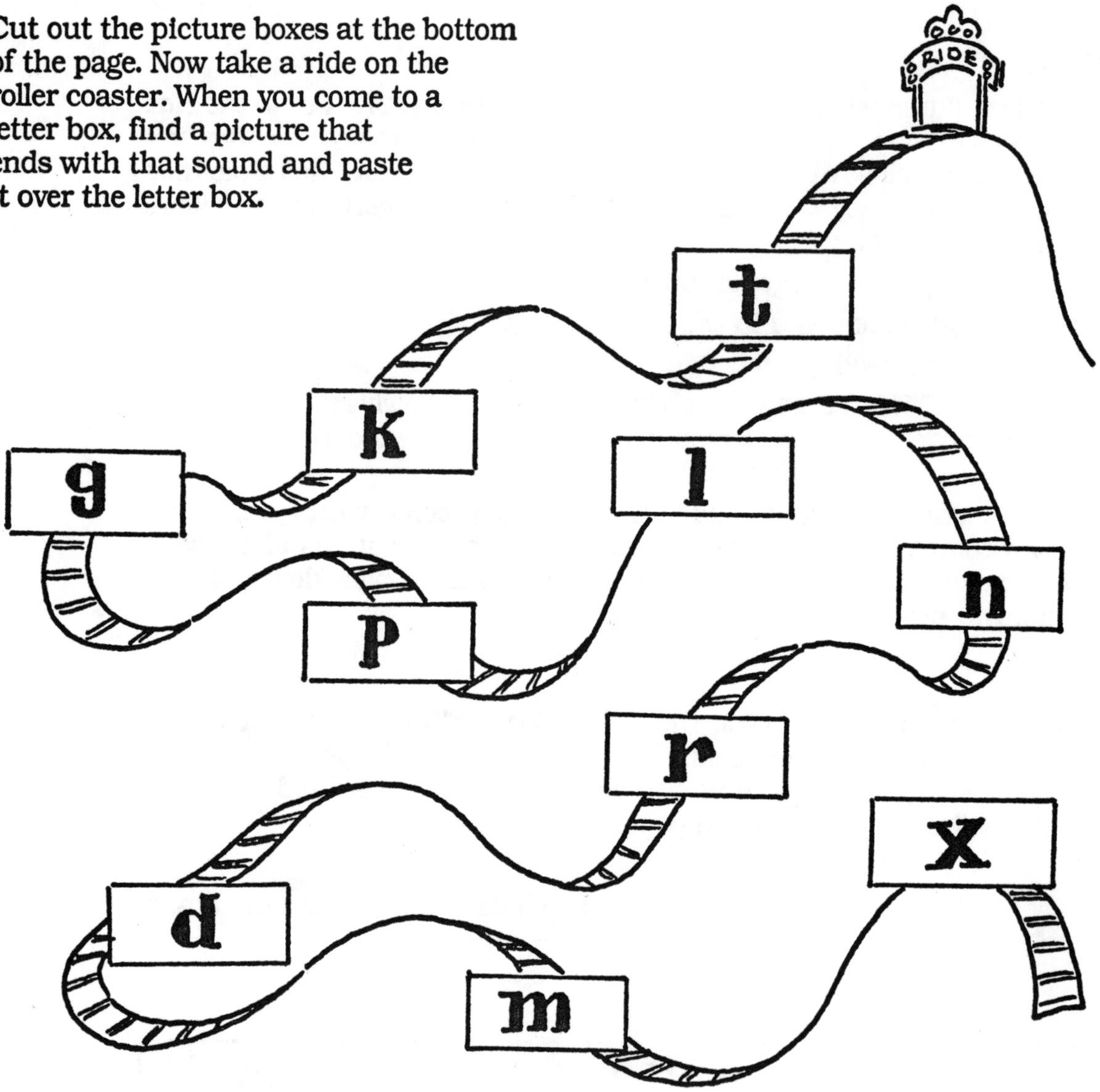

RIDE

t

k

g

l

n

p

r

x

d

m

SUGGESTION: It is advisable to do the first box together with your class so that everyone will understand the directions.

The activity sheet is easily corrected. Simply see that the following letters and items have been correctly matched:

t – bat	n – ten
k – sock	r – four
g – pig	d – bed
p – cap	m – broom
l – bell	x – box

Bulletin Boards/Displays for Skill Reinforcement

The following bulletin boards and displays have been designed to provide the students with meaningful practice in final consonant recognition.

Display Number One: Help Bert Mail the Letters

Materials Needed:

white background paper	white posterboard
felt-tipped pens (various colors)	thumbtacks
7 cereal boxes	stapler
blue construction paper	scissors
legal-size envelope	

Construction Directions:

1. Use the opaque projector to trace the lettering and figures onto the background paper.
2. Cover the cereal boxes with the blue construction paper. Mark and cut these boxes as shown here.

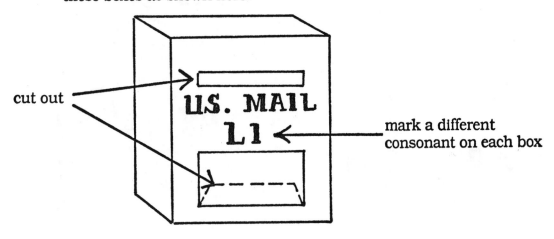

3. Mark the following pairs of letters, each on a different box, and attach them to the board:

   Ll, Tt, Pp, Dd, Mm, Nn, Gg

4. Cut and mark the white posterboard using the following envelope pattern:

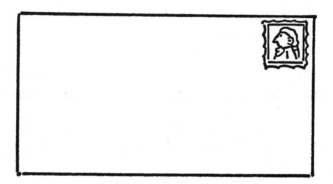

5. Mark the following drawings, each on a different envelope. Copy the corresponding letters on the back side of the envelopes:

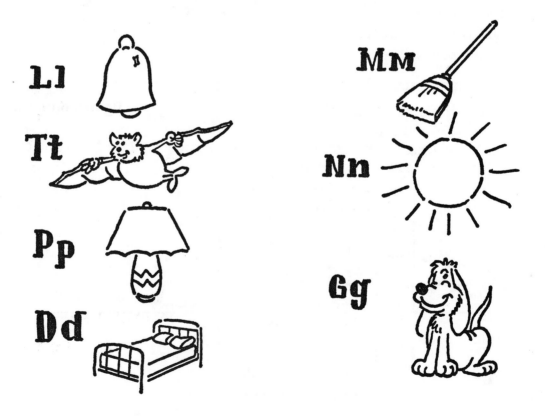

HELP BERT MAIL THE LETTERS

Directions:

1. Take the letters out of the envelope.
2. Look at the picture on one of them. What is the final sound? Can you find that letter on a mailbox? Mail it in that mailbox.
3. Do the same with all the letters.
4. When finished, turn over the letters to see if you were correct.

U.S. MAIL
Mm

U.S. MAIL
Tt

U.S. MAIL
Ll

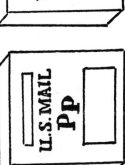

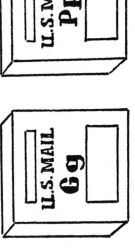

U.S. MAIL
Dd

U.S. MAIL
Pp

U.S. MAIL
Gg

U.S. MAIL
Nn

letters

6. Mark "letters" on the envelope, attach it to the board, and place all the letters in it.

Bulletin Board Use:

The children take the letters out of the envelope. They are to place each in the appropriate mailbox by matching the final consonant on the mailbox with the picture on the envelope. When they are finished, they may turn over the envelopes for the correct answer.

Display Number Two: Plant a Posy

Materials Needed:

white background paper
felt-tipped pens (various colors)
posterboard (various colors)
legal-size envelope
stapler
scissors

Construction Directions:

1. Use an opaque projector to trace the lettering and figures onto the background paper.
2. Cut and mark brown posterboard using an enlargement of the pot pattern shown here.

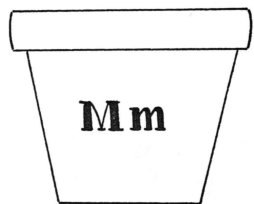

3. Mark the following letter pairs, each on a different pot. Attach them to the board by stapling the sides and bottom of each pot. Do not staple the top:

    Mm, Rr, Tt, Nn, Pp, Gg, Ll, Dd, Ss, Ff, Kk

4. Cut and mark the posterboard using an enlargement of the flower pattern shown here.

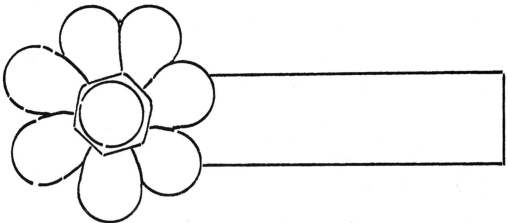

5. Draw each of the following pictures on a different flower. Copy the corresponding letter pair on the back side of each flower.

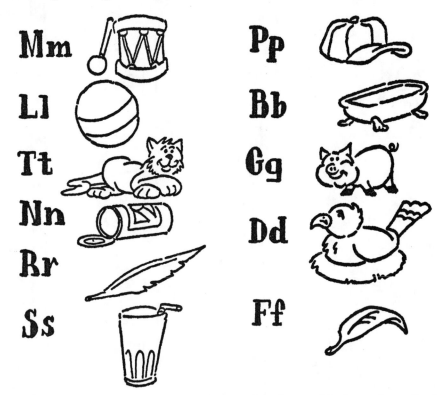

6. Print "flowers" on the envelope, attach to the board, and place the flowers in it.

Bulletin Board Use:

The children take the flowers out of the envelope and place each in the appropriate pot by matching the final consonant on the pot with the picture on the flower. When finished, they may turn over the flowers for the correct answer.

PLANT A POSY

Directions:

1. Take the flowers out of the envelope.
2. Look at the picture on one of them. What is the final sound? Can you find that letter on a pot? Plant it in that pot.
3. Do the same with all the flowers.
4. When you finish, turn over the flowers to see if you were correct.

Mm   Rr   Tt

Nn   Pp   Ss   Ff

Kk   Gg   Ll   Dd

flowers

Display Number Three: Lots of Lollypops

Materials Needed:

> large frozen juice cans
> posterboard (various colors)
> tongue depressors
> felt-tipped pens (various colors)
> scissors
> tape
> glue
> bright-colored self-stick vinyl
> hole punch

Construction Directions:

> 1. Make the lollypops by using the following instructions:

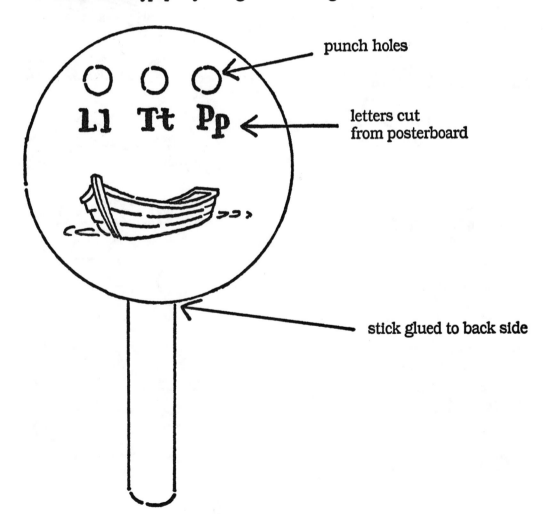

punch holes

letters cut
from posterboard

stick glued to back side

2. Mark the following letter pairs and drawings, each on the front of a different lollypop as shown in the illustration. Draw a circle around the correct letter hole on the "backside" of the lollypop.

Ll Tt Pp

Bb Pp Rr

Bb Gg Ff

Gg Dd Ff

Rr Mm Nn

Nn Hh Mm

Rr Pp Tt

Mm Tt Rr

Ss Bb Gg

Tt Cc Nn

3. Cover three juice cans with bright self-stick vinyl and place four lolly-pops in each.

4. Use an opaque projector to copy the following on a sheet of posterboard. Attach it over a counter and place the "jars of lollypops" in front of it.

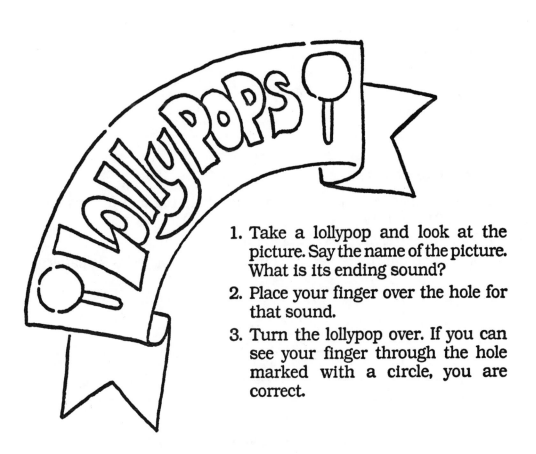

1. Take a lollypop and look at the picture. Say the name of the picture. What is its ending sound?

2. Place your finger over the hole for that sound.

3. Turn the lollypop over. If you can see your finger through the hole marked with a circle, you are correct.

Display Use:

The children choose a lollypop from the display and say the name of the picture on it. They are to place their finger over the letter hole representing that ending sound. By turning the lollypop over, they can quickly self-check their response by seeing whether their finger is visible through the marked hole.

Display Number Four: Crazy Caboose

Materials Needed:

background paper
straight pins
posterboard
felt-tipped pens (various colors)
scissors
stapler
hole punch
legal-size envelope
construction paper

Construction Directions:

1. Use an opaque projector to trace the lettering and figures onto the background paper.
2. Place the straight pins along the track as shown.
3. Mark and cut the posterboard into the following caboose pattern:

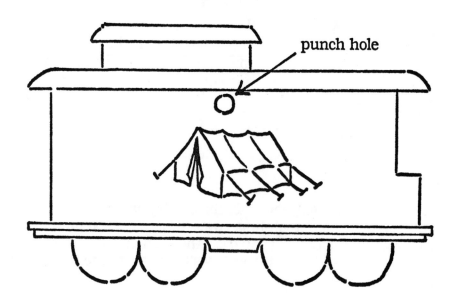

punch hole

4. Draw each of the following on a different caboose:

5. Mark "caboose" on the envelope, attach it to the board, and place the caboose cards in it.

6. Fold a sheet of construction paper and mark "Answer Key" on the cover. Copy the following on the inside and attach it to the board:

Bulletin Board Use:

The children are to take the caboose cards from the envelope and attempt to hang them on the hooks whose letter matches the final letter sound of the drawings on the caboose cards. They may use the Answer Key when finished.

Directions:

1. Take the cabooses out of the envelope.
2. Follow the crazy caboose's track. When you come to a letter box find a picture, on a caboose, that ends with that sound. Hang it on the hook. Do the same with all the cabooses.
3. Use the Answer Key when you finish.

CRAZY CABOOSE

Answer key

t

x

m

s

P

n

d

g

caboose

© 1998 by The Center for Applied Research in Education

MEDIAL VOWELS

Introductory Lesson

Objective

Children will be able to make the correct association between the vowels and their short sounds when in the medial position.

Materials Needed:

butcher paper
magazines/catalogs
ditto master
ditto paper
scissors
paste
chalkboard
objects whose name contains a short vowel

Introduction

Place an assortment of the following objects on a table or desk so all children can easily see:

hat, cap, bat, bag, pen, safety pin, can, rug,
bug, ring, stick, pig, fig, ship, bell, hen, sled,
jug, tub, bus, cup, gum, duck, box, doll, rock, sock,
lock, top
NOTE: Make substitutions for those objects as long as their name contains a short vowel.

Copy the following vowels on the chalkboard:

A   E   I   O   U

Ask the children to think of a word that contains a short a. Write a correct suggestion under the a. Do this with each of the vowels, making sure the children say both the word and the vowel sound for each one you write on the board.

Now tell the children that they will take turns coming to the table and selecting an object. They are then to walk to the appropriate vowel on the board, turn to the class, and say the name of the object. If they are correct, they may take the object back to their desk. If not, the object must be returned to the table. Do this until all objects have been successfully identified. Have them returned to the table.

Procedure:

Divide the class into small groups. Pass out magazines, scissors, paste, and butcher paper to each group. The children are now to cut out pictures from magazines whose names contain short vowels. They are to paste each picture on the butcher paper, slightly overlapping the edges to form a collage. When finished, each group should have a completed collage.

> SUGGESTION: You may want to make a small collage of pictures prior to introducing this activity so the children will more easily understand what they are to do.

Each group will then bring their finished collage to the front of the class, one at a time, and name off all the objects. You must keep a tally of these on the chalkboard. Whichever group has the most "different" objects is the winner.

Evaluation:

Use the activity sheet "The Kids" to see how well your children understand medial vowel letter/sound relationships.

Before distributing copies of the activity sheet, you should copy the following on the chalkboard or a transparency:

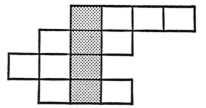

You can do this over a puddle.

You can do this with scissors.

You can write with it.

The sun does this at night.

WORD LIST

cut

set

pen

jump

Using the children's suggestions, write the answers in the spaces. Tell the children that if they are correct, the letters in the shaded squares will spell one of the months. (See the Answer Key.) When you think your students understand the procedure, distribute the activity sheet and let them begin. You should take note of those students having difficulty with this assignment and plan a special group session to reteach medial vowel letter/sound relationships.

```
ANSWER KEY
J    (j)ump
U    c(u)t
N    pe(n)
E    s(e)t
```

The activity sheet is self-correcting. As shown in the **Answer Key**, the shaded boxes will spell three children's names if the sheet is completed correctly.

```
ANSWER KEY
Puzzle One:
   B    (b)ed
   R    (r)ed
   E    b(e)ll
   N    ma(n)
   D    da(d)
   A    b(a)g
Puzzle Two:
   R    (r)ug
   I    l(i)d
   C    (c)up
   H    s(h)ut
   A    c(a)t
   R    t(r)ap
   D    (d)ig
Puzzle Three:
   W    (w)ell
   I    h(i)t
   L    hi(l)l
   L    c(l)ock
   I    sh(i)p
   A    m(a)p
   M    ha(m)
```

Name _____

Date _____

"I know the names of the kids in my class at school!" said John.

"Oh, I bet you don't," said Steve.

"I can name them all," said John.

"Bet you can't!" said Steve.

So John tried to name all the kids in his class, but he couldn't remember three. John needs help! Next to each puzzle is a Word List box. If you can find the answer to each riddle in the box, write it in the blanks. If you are correct, the letters in the shaded boxes will spell the names of the three kids John couldn't remember. Each puzzle will have its own answer.

Puzzle 1:

(1) You sleep in it.

(2) A color.

(3) You can ring it.

(4) A grown-up boy.

(5) Your father.

(6) You can put things in it.

WORD LIST
bell
dad
bed
red
man
bag

Puzzle 2:

(1) You put it on the floor.

(2) It covers a cooking pot.

(3) You drink from it.

(4) You can do it to a door.

(5) It goes "meow."

(6) You catch things with it.

(7) You do it with a shovel.

WORD LIST
cup
shut
rug
lid
dig
trap
cat

Puzzle 3:

(1) You get water from it.

(2) You do it with a bat.

(3) You can climb it.

(4) It helps you tell time.

(5) It floats on the water.

(6) It shows you where to go.

(7) You can eat it.

WORD LIST
hill
clock
map
ship
ham
well
hit

Bulletin Boards/Displays for Skill Reinforcement

The following bulletin boards and displays have been designed to provide the students with meaningful practice in medial vowel recognition.

Display Number One: Deep-Sea Diver

Materials Needed:

white background paper
blue cellophane
felt-tipped pens (various colors)
straight pins
stapler
blue construction paper
scissors
hole punch

Construction Directions:

1. Use an opaque projector to trace the figures and lettering onto the background paper.
2. Cut the blue construction paper using the following bubble pattern. You will need twenty-five bubbles.

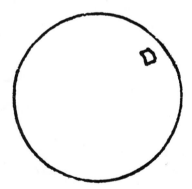

3. Copy each of the following drawings on a different bubble:

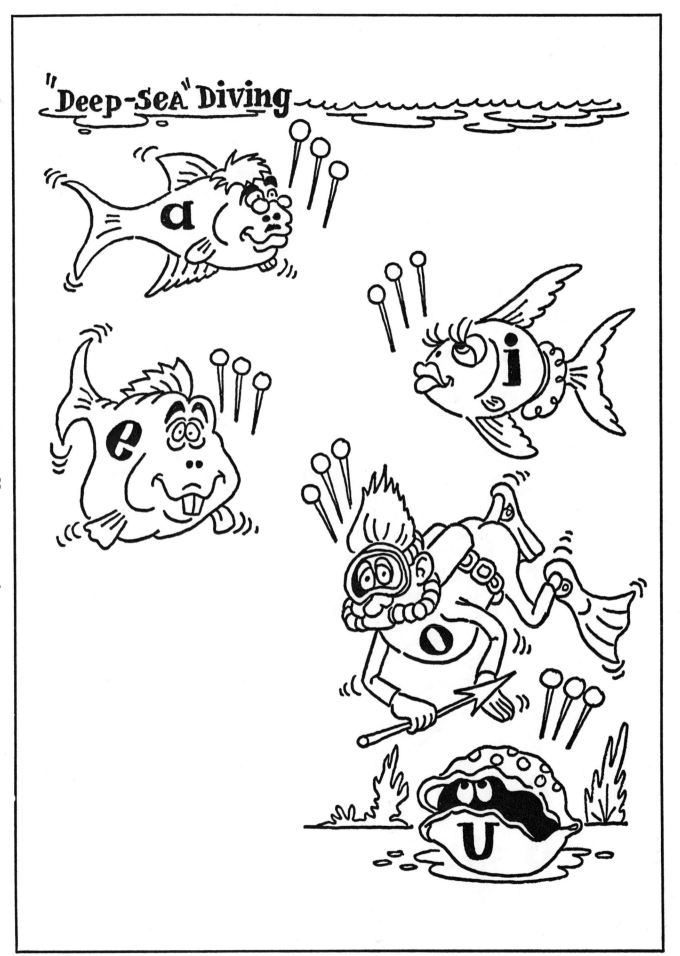

4. Cover the bulletin board with blue cellophane for a watery effect.

Bulletin Board Use:

Discuss the bulletin board with the students, pointing out the five "underwater vowel characters." Select five bubbles, each with a drawing containing a different medial vowel. Have various volunteers attach the five bubbles above the appropriate vowel character.

> SUGGESTION: Continue this activity over the next several days, using five additional vowel bubbles each time.

Display Number Two: Sip a Soda

Materials Needed:

white background paper	drinking straws
felt-tipped pens (various colors)	scissors
paper cups	tape
construction paper	stapler
legal-size envelope	

Construction Directions:

1. Use the opaque projector to trace the figures and lettering onto the background paper.
2. Attach the paper cups to the board as shown in the illustration.
3. Print the following vowels, each on a small piece of paper and tape one to each straw:

   a, i, o, u, e, i, e

4. Fold a sheet of construction paper, mark "Answer Key" on the cover, copy the following on the inside, and attach it to the board:

SIP A SODA

Directions:

1. Take the straws out of the envelope.
2. Look at one of the pictures. Say the word. What vowel sound do you hear?
3. Place that vowel straw in the cup under the picture that has the same vowel sound.
4. Do the same with all the straws.
5. When you finish you may use the Answer Key. Be sure to put the straws back in the envelope.

Answer Key

Straws

Bulletin Board Use:

Children take the straws out of the envelope and place them in the cups according to the medial vowels. When they are finished, they may use the Answer Key.

Display Number Three: Ride the Big Wheel

Materials Needed:

white background paper
white posterboard
felt-tipped pens (various colors)
construction paper
scissors
long thumbtack
stapler

Construction Directions:

1. Use an opaque projector to trace the lettering and figures onto the background paper.
2. Cut and mark the posterboard using an enlargement of the Ferris wheel pattern shown here.

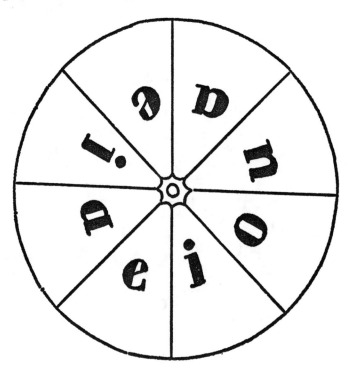

Directions:

1. Spin the wheel. What vowel has stopped between the legs of the Ferris wheel?

2. Look for an object on the board with that vowel sound.

3. When you find one, look in the Answer Key to see if you are correct.

RIDE THE BIG WHEEL

3. Attach the wheel to the board with a long thumbtack.

4. Fold a sheet of construction paper and mark "Answer Key" on the front. Copy the following on the inside and attach it to the board:

Bulletin Board Use:

The children spin the wheel and wait for it to stop. A vowel will be shown between the legs of the Ferris wheel. The children must then find a drawing of an object with that medial vowel sound. When finished, the children may use the Answer Key.

Display Number Four: Rough Sea

Materials Needed:

light blue background paper
construction paper (various colors)
felt-tipped pens (various colors)
scissors
stapler

Construction Directions:

1. Use an opaque projector to trace the lettering and figures onto the background paper.
2. Make a cut along each of the waves.
3. Cut the construction paper using the following boat pattern. You will need six.

4. Attach each of these by slipping them behind the waves.
5. Cut and mark the white construction paper using the sail pattern shown here.

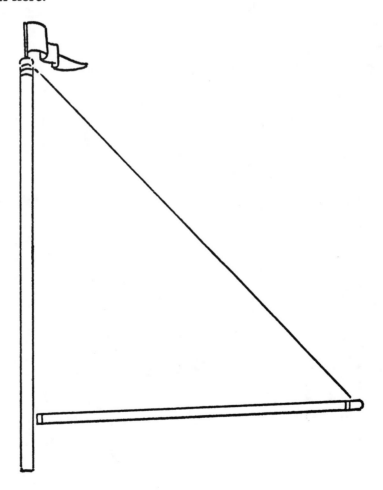

ROUGH SEA

Directions:

1. Look at the drawings on the different sails.
2. Do you know what vowel sound is in each? When you think you know, turn the sail over for the correct answer.

6. Copy the following drawings, each on a different sail, and attach one to each of the boats. Mark the corresponding vowel behind each sail for the self-check.

Bulletin Board Use:

The children say the word for the picture on each sail and determine the vowel which is sounded. When they think they know, they may turn the sail over for the self-check.

CONSONANT BLENDS

Introductory Lesson

Objective:

The children will be able to make the correct association between selected consonant blends and their sounds when given in the initial position.

Materials Needed:

chalkboard	ditto paper
ditto master	posterboard

brad   scissors
felt-tipped pen   note cards

Introduction:

Use the posterboard and brad to make the following spinner. Enlarge it to approximately two feet in diameter.

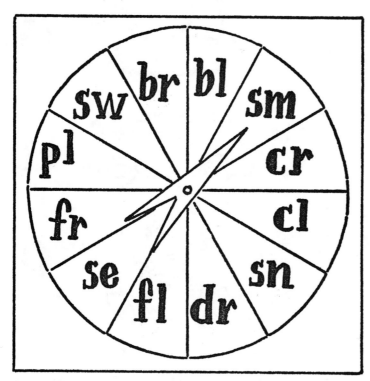

cut arrow from posterboard

attach posterboard arrow with brad

Divide your students into three teams. Have them select names and then copy these on the chalkboard for scorekeeping purposes. Each team will take turns sending a member to spin the blend wheel. This person must correctly say a word beginning with the blend shown on the spinner and may not have help from anyone else. If the student succeeds, his or her team receives five points. If not, no points are given, and it becomes the next team's turn. When all members from each team have participated, the game is over. The team with the highest score is the winner.

NOTE: No player should be allowed to use a word already used for a particular blend.

Procedure:

Copy the following blend/words, each on a different notecard:

BRing	FLy	CLimb	SPin	SNeeze
BRight	SMell	CLown	STop	SCare

BRidge	FRog	SMall	STick	SKip
BRave	FReeze	PLay	STep	SWim
CRy	GRab	SLeep	DRag	TWist
CRawl	PRetty	SLip	SMile	DRaw
CRow	TRain	SPeak	SMooth	GLove
DRink	BLow			

Tell the children they are now going to play the "Blendomime Game." This is accomplished by acting out (pantomime fashion) words beginning with consonant blends. Each child will select a card, making sure not to show it to any classmate. The first player will then:

(1) print the blend on the chalkboard,

(2) pantomime the word, and

(3) have other children try to guess the word.

When the correct word is guessed another child selects a card and the game continues in the same fashion.

> SUGGESTION: It is advisable for you to select one of the words and go through the procedure first so all children will easily understand what is expected of them.

Evaluation:

Use the activity sheet "Mouse Match" to see how well your children understand initial consonant blend letter/sound relationships. Before distributing copies of the activity sheet, you should copy the following on the chalkboard:

tr

sl

br

Using the children's suggestions, draw lines from the blends to the drawings beginning with those blends. (See the Answer Key.) When you think your students understand the procedure, distribute the activity sheet and let them begin. You should take note of those children having difficulty with this assignment and plan a special group session to reteach selected consonant blends.

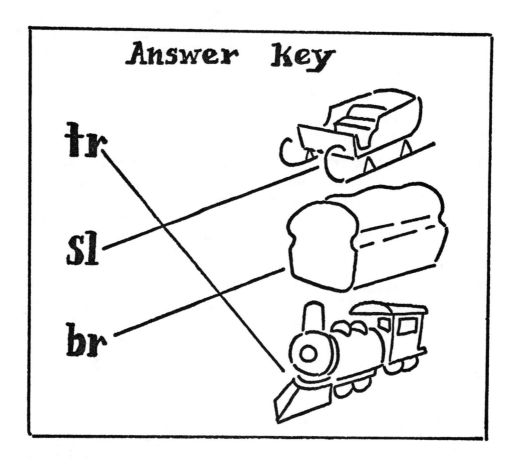

The activity sheet is easily corrected. Simply see that the following matches have been made.

tr – tree	sp – spoon
br – brush	sn – snake
cl – cloud	gr – grape
sm – smoke	

Mouse MATCH

Name _____

Date _____

Match the mice with the cheese. Draw a line from a mouse with a blend sound to the cheese showing an object that begins with that blend sound.

Bulletin Boards/Displays for Skill Reinforcement

The following bulletin boards and displays have been designed to provide the students with meaningful practice in consonant blend recognition.

Display Number One: I Vont You!

Materials Needed:

white background paper
felt-tipped pens (various colors)
gray construction paper
scissors
stapler

Construction Directions:

1. Use an opaque projector to trace the lettering and figures onto the background paper. Use the felt-tipped pens and color appropriately.

2. Cut the gray construction paper using the following bat pattern. You will need twelve.

3. Mark the following blend/picture groups, each on a different bat as shown in the illustrations:

4. Attach the bats to the board and mark "correct" and "wrong" on the board behind the appropriate bat wings.

Bulletin Board Use:

Children are to look at the consonant blend on each bat and decide which drawing on the bat begins with that blend. They are to flip up the wings to see if they are correct.

Directions:

1. Look at the blend on one of the bats.

2. Which of the items on his wings begins with that blend?

3. Look under that wing to see if you are right.

4. Keep doing this with all the bats.

YOU! YOU!

Display Number Two: Bucket of Blends

Materials Needed:

  a bright-color plastic pail
  posterboard
  hole punch
  tape
  felt-tipped pens (various colors)
  shoelaces
  scissors

Construction Directions:

1. Mark, fold, and cut the posterboard using the following pattern. Place it on the pail as shown in the illustration:

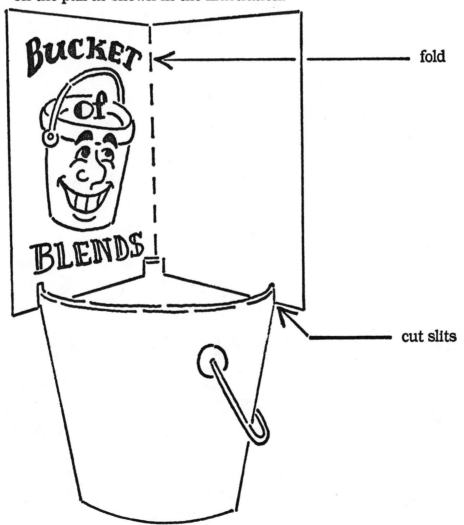

2. Cut, mark, and punch holes in the posterboard using the pattern shown here. Attach a shoelace to each piece.

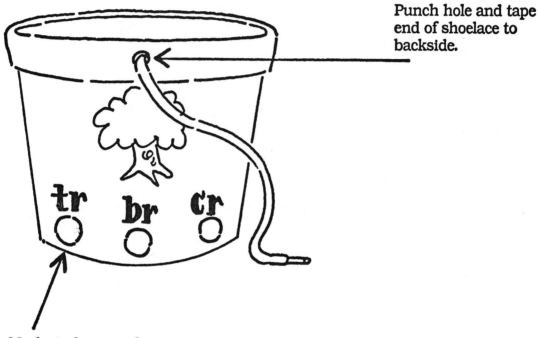

Punch hole and tape end of shoelace to backside.

Mark circle around the backside of the correct hole

3. Mark the following picture and blend groups, each on a different bucket as shown in the illustration:

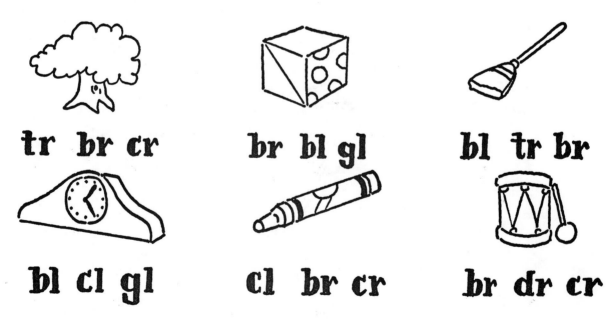

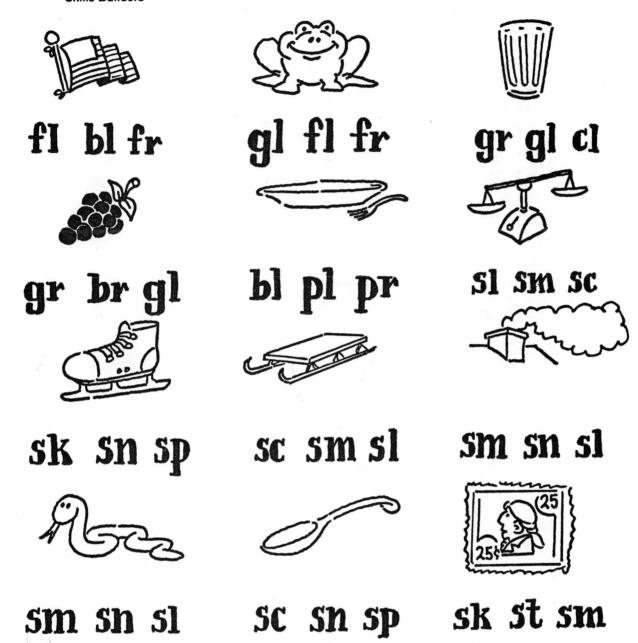

fl bl fr   gl fl fr   gr gl cl

gr br gl   bl pl pr   sl sm sc

sk sn sp   sc sm sl   sm sn sl

sm sn sl   sc sn sp   sk st sm

4. Place the playing card buckets in the pail.

Display Use:

The children take out a bucket card. They are to say the name of the picture, listening for the initial consonant blend sound. They place the shoelace through the hole under that sound. They may turn over the card for the self-check.

Display Number Three: Spin-A-Blend

Materials Needed:

> large cardboard box
> self-stick vinyl
> posterboard
> construction paper
> large brad
> scissors
> felt-tipped pen
> glue
> tape
> small items beginning with blends

Construction Directions:

1. Cover the cardboard box with self-stick vinyl.
2. Cut and mark the posterboard using an enlargement of the wheel pattern shown here.

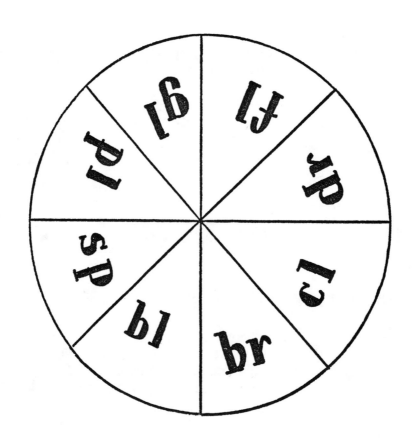

3. Attach this wheel to the box using the brad as shown here.

   IMPORTANT: Cut two small circles from the posterboard scraps and attach between the wheel and the box. These will act as washers and help it spin freely.

4. Cut and mark the posterboard using the arrow and directions patterns shown here. Attach them to the box as shown in the illustration.

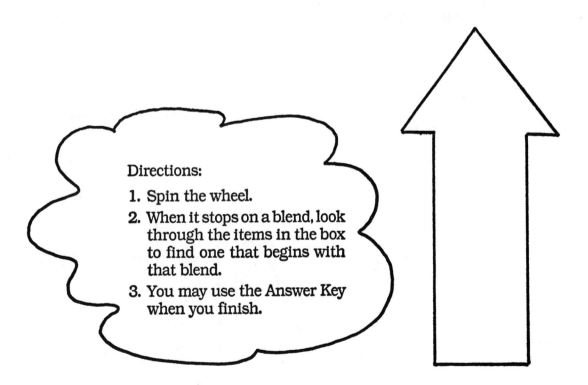

Directions:

1. Spin the wheel.
2. When it stops on a blend, look through the items in the box to find one that begins with that blend.
3. You may use the Answer Key when you finish.

5. Place in the box one item beginning with the following blends:

BL (block)   BR (broom)
CL (clock)   DR (drum)
FL (flag, flower)   GL (glove, glass)
PL (plate)   SP (spoon)

6. Fold a sheet of construction paper and mark "Answer Key" on the cover. Mark the blends on the inside along with their matching box items. Attach this to the side of the box.

Display Use:

The children are to spin the wheel and find an item in the box that begins with the consonant blend that stops on the arrow. They may use the Answer Key when they finish.

Display Number Four: Dangerous Dive

Materials Needed:

heavy posterboard   construction paper
scissors   small basket
felt-tipped pens (various colors)   glue
seven wooden pincher clothespins   tape
small throw rug

Construction Directions:

1. Mark and cut a large sheet of heavy posterboard using an enlargement of the pattern shown here. Then cut and attach a piece of heavyweight posterboard to hold up the display.

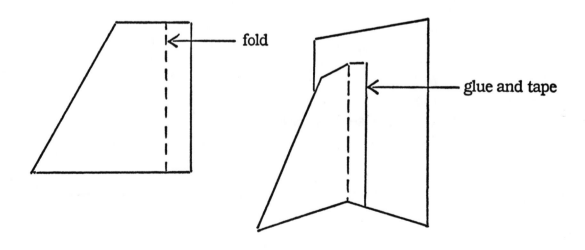

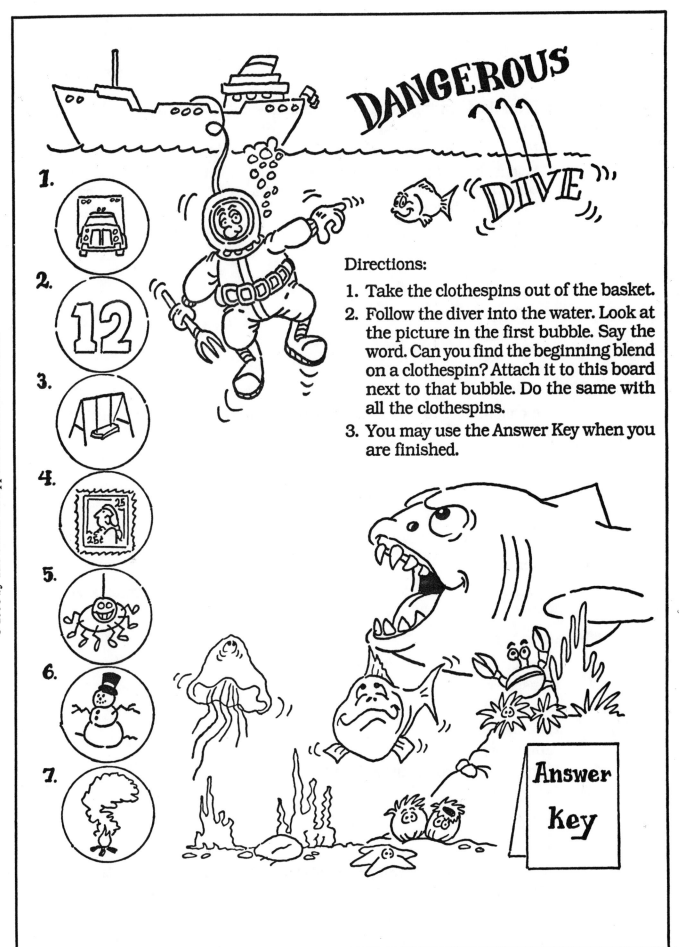

DANGEROUS DIVE

Directions:

1. Take the clothespins out of the basket.
2. Follow the diver into the water. Look at the picture in the first bubble. Say the word. Can you find the beginning blend on a clothespin? Attach it to this board next to that bubble. Do the same with all the clothespins.
3. You may use the Answer Key when you are finished.

1.

2.

3.

4.

5.

6.

7.

Answer Key

2. Print the following blends, each on a different clothespin:
   tr, tw, sw, st, sp, sn, sm
3. Place these in a basket on a small rug in front of the display.
4. Fold a sheet of construction paper, mark "Answer Key" on the front, copy the following on the inside, and attach to the board as shown in the illustration.
   (1) tr
   (2) tw
   (3) sw
   (4) st
   (5) sp
   (6) sn
   (7) sm

Display Use:

The children are to attach the clothespins next to the correct picture bubbles according to consonant blends. They may use the Answer Key when they finish.

CONTRACTIONS

Introductory Lesson

Objective:

Children will be able to make the correct association between selected contractions and the words they represent.

Materials Needed:

tape recorder
transparency
chalkboard
ditto master
ditto paper
bingo markers (corn, buttons, etc.)
felt-tipped pen
scissors

Introduction:

Tell the children you have taped a story you want them to listen to. Play the following story which you previously recorded:

"It is gone again!" yelled Al Seth.

He was panting from the long run he had just made. His mother, father, and younger brother, Brian, all came out of the cottage to see what was the matter.

"Well, tell us about it," said Mr. Seth.

"You are not going to believe it! It is just like it was yesterday and the two times before that," said Al. "The boat has disappeared again. Brian was with me when I tied it up. He knows that I was extra careful this time. You could not have tied it better yourself, Dad!"

"Al is right," replied Brian. "I helped him with it! We were not careless!"

"Well then, this *is* a mystery," said Mr. Seth. "I guess we will just have to go looking for it again. We might as well begin over at the mill stream, since that is where we have found it before."

The Seths were on their vacation at Marble Island. They had been on the island for one week. During this time their boat had turned up missing three times. This time made the fourth. Every evening they tied it to the dock, but for the past three mornings it was gone.

"Here it is!" called Brian. "Just as we found it the other times."

Al and Brian pulled the boat back to the dock. As they finished tying it securely in place, Mr. Seth said, "Here is what we are going to do. Tonight after dark, Al and I will not go to bed as we usually do. Instead, we will quietly creep down to the brush near the boat dock. We will wait there and try to find out who it is that has been fooling with our boat."

The sun had not disappeared too long before Al and his Dad were hiding in the brush near the boat dock. They had not been waiting long before they heard a noise. Someone was on the dock at that very minute. Mr. Seth aimed his flashlight at the boat and yelled, "Who is out there?"

A loud splash was heard as Al and his Dad raced out on the dock. Then Mr. Seth began laughing and pointing out in the water. There swimming for all he was worth was Ringo, the Alexander's pet dog.

Mrs. Seth and Brian had come running when they had heard the noise. So there stood all four of the Seths on the dock laughing at their mysterious visitor, frantically swimming home.

Now explain that you recorded the same story again but made certain changes. They are to listen and see if they can guess what the changes are. Play the following story which you previously recorded. Note the changes in the contractions:

"It's gone again!" yelled Al Seth.

He was panting from the long run he'd just made. His mother, father, and younger brother, Brian, all came out of the cottage to see what was the matter.

"Well, tell us about it," said Mr. Seth.

"You're not going to believe it! It's just like it was yesterday and the two times before that," said Al. "The boat has disappeared again. Brian was with me when I tied it up. He knows that I was extra careful this time. You couldn't have tied it better yourself, Dad!"

"Al's right," replied Brian. "I helped him with it! We weren't careless!"

"Well then, this *is* a mystery," said Mr. Seth. "I guess we'll just have to go looking for it again. We might as well begin over at the mill stream, since that's where we've found it before."

The Seths were on their vacation at Marble Island. They'd been on the island for one week. During this time their boat had turned up missing three times. This time made the fourth. Every evening they tied it to the dock, but for the past three mornings it was gone.

"Here it is!" called Brian. "Just as we found it the other times."

Al and Brian pulled the boat back to the dock. As they finished tying it securely in place, Mr. Seth said, "Here's what we are going to do. Tonight after dark, Al and I won't go to bed as we usually do. Instead, we'll quietly creep down to the brush near the boat dock. We'll wait there and try to find out who it is that has been fooling with our boat."

The sun had not disappeared too long before Al and his Dad were hiding in the brush near the boat dock. They'd not been waiting long before they heard a noise. Someone was on the dock at that very minute. Mr. Seth aimed his flashlight at the boat and yelled, "Who's out there?"

A loud splash was heard as Al and his Dad raced out on the dock. Then Mr. Seth began laughing and pointing out in the water. There swimming for all he was worth was Ringo, the Alexander's pet dog.

Mrs. Seth and Brian had come running when they'd heard the noise. So there stood all four of the Seths on the dock laughing at their mysterious visitor, frantically swimming home.

Ask the children what changes were made in the second version of the story. If no one suggests contractions then you should. Read the first sentence from each version as an example.

Write the following on the board:

> It is
>
> It's

Explain that a contraction is a single word formed by combining two words but omitting a letter or letters. An apostrophe is always inserted where a letter or letters have been omitted.

Now replay the second version of the story while the children write down as many of the contractions as they can hear. When finished copy their suggestions on the chalkboard. (See the Answer Key.)

ANSWER KEY	
it's	here's
you're	won't
couldn't	we'll
weren't	hadn't
we've	who's
he'd	they'd
Al's	we're
that's	

Procedure:

Tell the children they are going to play Contraction Bingo. You will need to do the following prior to game play:

(1) Duplicate copies of this gameboard. Each player will need one.

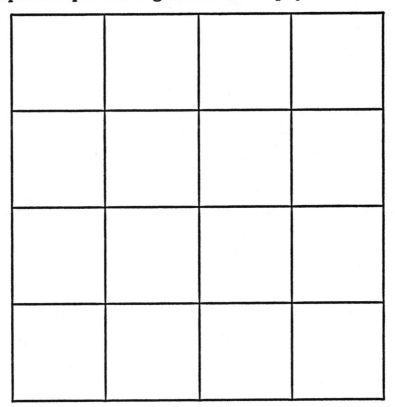

(2) Copy the following on a transparency or on the chalkboard:

I'm	let's	don't	hadn't
you're	I'd	isn't	mustn't
we're	you'd	won't	didn't
they're	he'd	shouldn't	I'll
he's	she'd	couldn't	you'll
she's	we'd	wouldn't	she'll
it's	they'd	aren't	he'll
what's	I've	doesn't	it'll
that's	you've	wasn't	we'll
who's	we've	weren't	they'll
there's	they've	hasn't	that'll
here's	can't	haven't	

(3) Pass out the gameboards and game markers to each player.

Now explain the rules of the game to the children. They are:

Each player must fill in a gameboard by copying the contractions, found on the transparency, in the gameboard squares. They may use each only once and may place them in any order.

NOTE: They will not be able to use all the contractions listed, only sixteen.

As you read through the following list of words, players are to cover the corresponding contractions on their gameboards.

SUGGESTION: Skip around the list and place a mark next to those words read. This will also help in verifying the winner.

The first player to correctly place four markers in a straight row (horizontal, vertical, or diagonal) should say BINGO. This player is the winner.

BINGO WORD LIST

I am	she would	has not
you are	we had	have not
we are	they had	had not
they are	I have	must not
he is	you have	did not
she is	we have	I will
it is	they have	you will
what is	can not	she will
that is	do not	he will
who is	is not	it will
there is	would not	we will
here is	should not	they will
let us	could not	that will
I would	are not	does not
you had	was not	were not
he had		

Evaluation:

Use the activity sheet "Captain Clod" to see how well your children understand contraction usage.

Before distributing copies of the activity sheet, you should copy the following on the chalkboard:

she's	he will
it's	she is
he'll	it is

Ask a volunteer to color the concentration boxes each a different color, using colored chalk. Now select other volunteers to match the word boxes with the contraction boxes by coloring them the same colors. (See the Answer Key.) When you think your students understand the procedure, distribute the activity sheet and let them begin. You should take note of those students having difficulty with this assignment and plan a special group session to reteach contractions.

ANSWER KEY

she's	she is
it's	it is
he'll	he will

Name _____

Date _____

CAPTAIN CLOD

Follow Captain Clod as he flies through the city in search of criminals. First color each contraction box a different color. Now, start at Captain Clod and follow his path. When you come to a word box, look through the contraction boxes for the correct one. When you find it, color the word box with the same color as the contraction box. Continue to do this until Captain Clod reaches the criminal.

you're

he's

I've

that'll

we've

weren't

can't

isn't

it'll

I'll

can not

were not

we have

you are

I will

he is

it will

I have

that will

is not

The activity sheet is easily corrected. Simply make sure the words and their corresponding contractions are colored in pairs matching the Answer Key.

ANSWER KEY	
you're	you are
he's	he is
I've	I have
that'll	that will
we've	we have
weren't	were not
can't	can not
isn't	is not
it'll	it will
I'll	I will

Bulletin Boards/Displays for Skill Reinforcement

The following bulletin boards and displays have been designed to provide the students with meaningful practice in contraction usage.

Display Number One: Twig Twirl

Materials Needed:

white background paper
tan posterboard
long thumbtack
felt-tipped pens (various colors)
small gelatin boxes
glue
scissors
green construction paper
stapler

Construction Directions:

1. Use an opaque projector to trace, cut, and mark the "title twig" from the tan posterboard. Attach the small gelatin boxes to the board and glue the twig to these. This will give a three-dimensional effect.

Directions:

1. Twirl the twig.
2. When it stops, look for a leaf that has a word to match.
3. When you finish use the Answer Key.

Answer Key

I'll

it's

isn't

I'm

can't

don't

I'd

didn't

Twig Twirl

is not

I will

it is

I would

did not

I am

cannot

do not

© 1998 by The Center for Applied Research in Education

2. Use an opaque projector to trace the figures and lettering onto the background paper.

3. Mark and cut out the twig spinner from the posterboard and attach it to the board with a long thumbtack.

4. Fold a sheet of green construction paper to form an Answer Key and mark the front cover as shown. Mark the following on the inside and attach to the board:

do not – don't	did not – didn't
I would – I'd	it is – it's
I will – I'll	can not – can't
is not – isn't	I am – I'm

Bulletin Board Use:

Children spin the twig. When it stops on the two words they must look for their appropriate contraction. When they finish, they may use the Answer Key to correct themselves.

Display Number Two: Three-Alarm Fire

Materials Needed:

background paper
felt-tipped pens (various colors)
posterboard
scissors
legal-size envelope
library-book card pockets
stapler

Construction Directions:

1. Use an opaque projector to trace the lettering and figures onto the background paper.

2. Attach the book card pockets to the board as shown in the illustration. Print the following contractions, in order, each on a different pocket. Follow the path of the fire engine as you mark the pockets.

I've	who'll
doesn't	who'd
can't	you'd
shouldn't	

3. Cut and mark the posterboard using the ladder pattern shown here. You will need seven ladders.

4. Copy each of the following on a different ladder. Be sure to circle the letters that are circled in this list:

I h(a)ve   wh(o) will

doe(s) not   who w(o)uld

(c)an not   you wou(l)d

s(h)ould not

5. Mark "ladders" on the envelope, attach it to the board, and place the ladders in it.

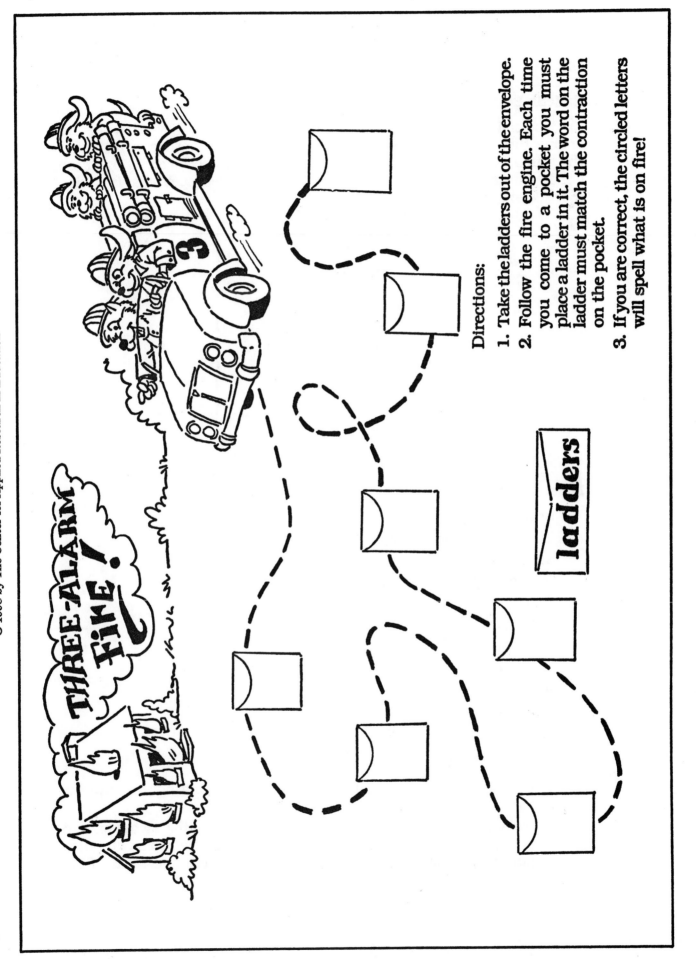

THREE-ALARM FIRE!

Directions:

1. Take the ladders out of the envelope.
2. Follow the fire engine. Each time you come to a pocket you must place a ladder in it. The word on the ladder must match the contraction on the pocket.
3. If you are correct, the circled letters will spell what is on fire!

ladders

Bulletin Board Use:

The children take the ladders out of the envelope. As they follow the fire engine, they are to place the appropriate ladders in the pockets by matching the words with the contractions. The bulletin board is self-correcting. If the children are correct, the circled letters on the ladders will spell what is on fire. (See the Answer Key.)

```
┌─────────────────────────────────────┐
│            ANSWER KEY                │
│                                      │
│     A       I h(a)ve                 │
│                                      │
│     S       doe(s) not               │
│                                      │
│     C       (c)an not                │
│                                      │
│     H       s(h)ould not             │
│                                      │
│     O       wh(o) will               │
│                                      │
│     O       who w(o)uld              │
│                                      │
│     L       you wou(l)d              │
└─────────────────────────────────────┘
```

Display Number Three: Arnold the Armadillo

Materials Needed:

orange background paper
black construction paper
straight pins
felt-tipped pens (various colors)
ditto box
ditto master
ditto paper
scissors
tape
stapler
brown construction paper

Construction Directions:

1. Use an opaque projector to trace the lettering and figures onto the background paper.

2. Mark and cut the black construction paper using the cactus pattern shown in the illustration. Attach it using the straight pins and then pull the form away from the board to give it a three-dimensional effect.

ARNOLD THE ARMADILLO

Complete one of my sheets and find out where I live!

Arnold's Sheets

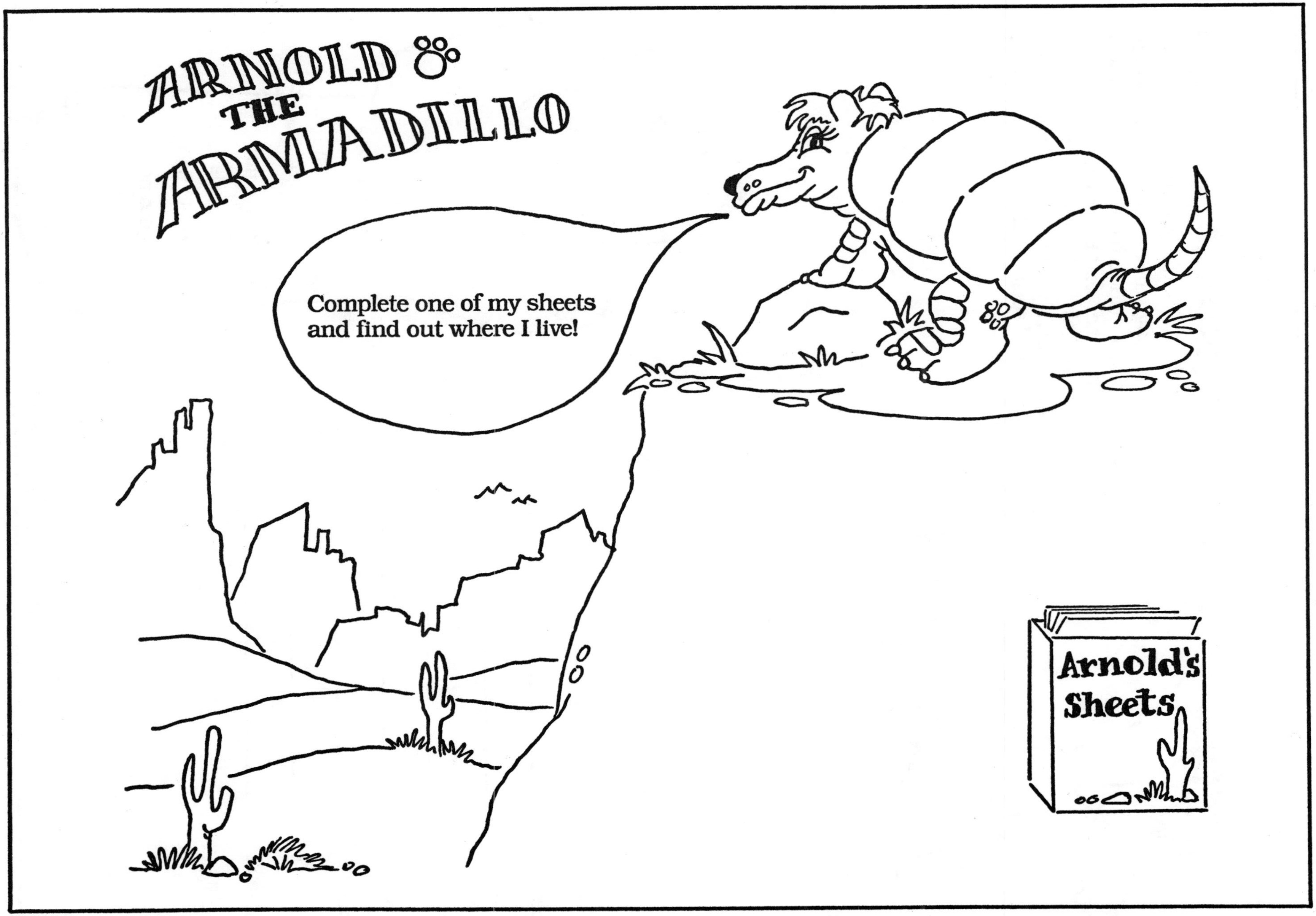

Name _____

Date _____

ARNOLD THE ARMADILLO

Below is a list of contractions. You are to look through the cactus to find the words each contraction represents. Write them on the space next to the contractions. Be sure to circle the letters that are circled in the cactus. If you are correct, these circled letters will spell where Arnold lives. Write it below.

there's _____

here's _____

she's _____

doesn't _____

aren't _____

wasn't _____

haven't _____

weren't _____

wouldn't _____

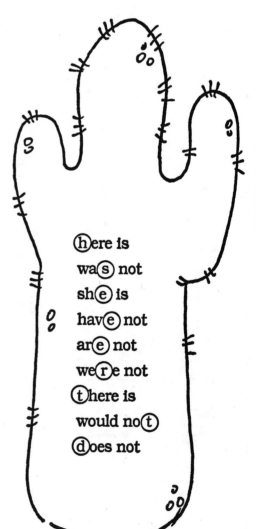

(h)ere is

wa(s) not

sh(e) is

hav(e) not

ar(e) not

we(r)e not

(t)here is

would no(t)

(d)oes not

_ _ _ _ _ _ _ _ _ _ _ _ _

3. Cut the ditto box in half across the width, cover with the brown construction paper, print "Arnold's Sheets" on the front, and attach it to the board.

4. Make copies of the "Arnold the Armadillo" activity sheet and place a supply in the bulletin board box.

Bulletin Board Use:

The children take an activity sheet and match the contractions with the words they represent. If they are correct, the circled letters will spell where Arnold the Armadillo lives. (See the Answer Key.)

```
          ANSWER KEY
   T      (t)here is
   H      (h)ere is
   E      sh(e) is

   D      (d)oes not
   E      ar(e) not
   S      wa(s) not
   E      hav(e) not
   R      we(r)e not
   T      would no(t)
```

Display Number Four: Crocodile Contractions

Materials Needed:

background paper
construction paper
posterboard
straight pins
felt-tipped pens (various colors)
legal-size envelope
stapler
hole punch
scissors

Construction Directions:

1. Use an opaque projector to trace the lettering and figures onto the background paper.

2. Cut, fold, and attach the dark green construction paper as shown here.

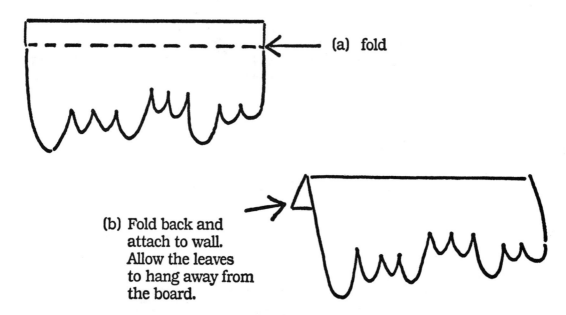

(a) fold

(b) Fold back and attach to wall. Allow the leaves to hang away from the board.

3. Place the straight pins on the board as shown in the illustration.

4. Cut and mark the posterboard using an enlargement of the following crocodile pattern. You will need seven.

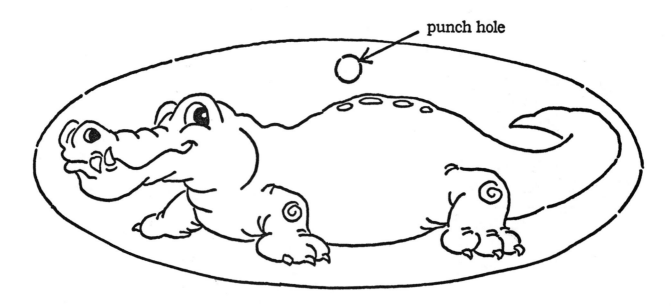

punch hole

would not

does not

had not

crocodiles

Answer Key

should not

can't not

do not

could not

BEWARE SWAMP

Directions:

1. Take the crocodiles out of the envelope.
2. Match them with the words on the board. Hang them on the appropriate hooks.
3. Use the Answer Key when you are finished.

5. Print each of the following contractions on a different crocodile:

can't	shouldn't
couldn't	wouldn't
don't	doesn't
hadn't	

6. Print "crocodiles" on the envelope and attach to the board. Place the crocodiles in it.

7. Fold a sheet of construction paper and mark "Answer Key" on the cover. Print the following on the inside and attach it to the board:

can not – can't	had not – hadn't
should not – shouldn't	would not – wouldn't
could not – couldn't	do not – don't
does not – doesn't	

Bulletin Board Use:

The children match the contractions on the crocodiles to the words on the board. They do this by hanging the crocodile pieces on the appropriate board hooks. They may use the Answer Key when they finish.

COMPOUND WORDS

Introductory Lesson

Objectives:

Children will be able to readily recognize selected compound words.

Children will be able to combine words in order to form selected compound words.

Materials Needed:

chalkboard
transparency
scissors
magazines/catalogs
paste
ditto master
ditto paper
background paper for bulletin board
stapler
felt-tipped pen

Introduction:

Copy the following short story on a transparency:

New Orleans is a beautiful city. It is one of the few cities that still has you can ride. On nice days you can look out on the harbor and watch many and dancing in the waves.

New Orleans is also an important seaport. On any day you can see great ships bringing goods, such as , into our country. During the night the faithful shines its light, directing ships to safety. In the early morning, at the first break of the port once again comes alive. Much seafood is available in the small ships along the harbor. Shrimp, clams, turtle, and even may be purchased.

Read through this story together with the class, having students read the picture words. After having read this, ask the students what all of the picture words have in common. When someone guesses they are all compound words point out that compound words are formed by combining two words. Now go back through the story and write each picture word on the chalkboard. You may want to have volunteers from the class do this. The appropriate compound words are:

STREETCARS	LIGHTHOUSE
SAILBOATS	DAYLIGHT
MOTORBOATS	SWORDFISH
PINEAPPLES	

Procedure:

Make a transparency of the next page by using a thermal transparency on your school's copier.

Tell the children that each of the picture pairs on the transparency will form a compound word. Ask for a volunteer to say what the first one might be. After receiving a correct response, write FISHHOOK after the equals sign. The children are to do the rest individually. (See the Answer Key.) After adequate time, ask volunteers to suggest the compound words as you write them on the transparency.

```
┌─────────────────────────────────────────┐
│              ANSWER KEY                   │
│   fishhook          frogman               │
│   rainbow           grasshopper           │
│   basketball        lipstick              │
│   buttercup         moonwalk              │
│   cowboy            pinball               │
│   pancake           screwdriver           │
│   ferryboat                               │
└─────────────────────────────────────────┘
```

Tell the children they are now to cut out pictures from magazines and paste them on a sheet of paper to form one of these "Compound Equations." These will be attached to a bulletin board for others to try and guess the compound word.

NOTE: Print the caption "Guess Our Compound Equations" on the background paper and attach the children's work.

You may want to copy a few of the following compound words on the chalkboard in order to stimulate ideas:

afternoon	dragonfly	paperback
anchorman	drawbridge	peppermint
ashtray	earring	railroad
backyard	eyeball	rattlesnake
billfold	football	sandpaper
bloodhound	fruitcake	shortstop
breakfast	goldfish	sidewalk
bulldog	haircut	skateboard
buttermilk	headlight	splashdown
campfire	highchair	sunflower
carpool	jellyfish	sweatshirt
clipboard	landlady	teacup
cupboard	motorcycle	timetable
daydream	outfield	toothbrush
downstairs	overcoat	waterfall

Evaluation:

Use the activity sheet "Take a Ride on the Streetcar!" to see how well your students recognize compound words. Before distributing copies of the activity sheet, you should copy the following on the chalkboard or a transparency:

bare _____

base _____

bed _____

```
┌─────────────────┐
│  WORD BOX       │
│  sp(r)ead       │
│  b(a)ll         │
│  ba(c)k         │
└─────────────────┘
```

Using the students' suggestions, fill in the words on the spaces, from the Word Box, to make compound words. Be sure to circle the letters that are circled in the Word Box. Point out that these letters will spell something if they are correct. (See the Answer Key.) When you think your students understand the procedure, distribute the activity sheet and let them begin. You should take note of those children having difficulty with this assignment and plan a special group session to reteach the selected compound words.

```
┌─────────────────────┐
│   ANSWER KEY        │
│  C   bareba(c)k     │
│  A   baseb(a)ll     │
│  R   bedsp(r)ead    │
└─────────────────────┘
```

The activity sheet is self-correcting. As shown in the answer key, the name NEW ORLEANS will be spelled if the sheet is completed correctly.

```
┌──────────────────────────────────────────────┐
│               ANSWER KEY                      │
│  N   afternoo(n)        O   barefo(o)t        │
│  E   windshi(e)ld       R   typewrite(r)      │
│  W   any(w)ay           L   anthi(l)l         │
│                         E   bookcas(e)        │
│                         A   salesm(a)n        │
│                         N   overgrow(n)       │
│                         S   swordfi(s)h       │
└──────────────────────────────────────────────┘
```

TAKE A RIDE
ON THE STREETCAR!

Name _____

Date _____

Get on the streetcar and take a ride. When you come to a sign, look through the Word List to find a word that, when combined with the sign, will make a compound word. When you find the word, write it on the space and circle the letter. If you are correct, the circled letters will spell the name of a city where you can still ride a streetcar.

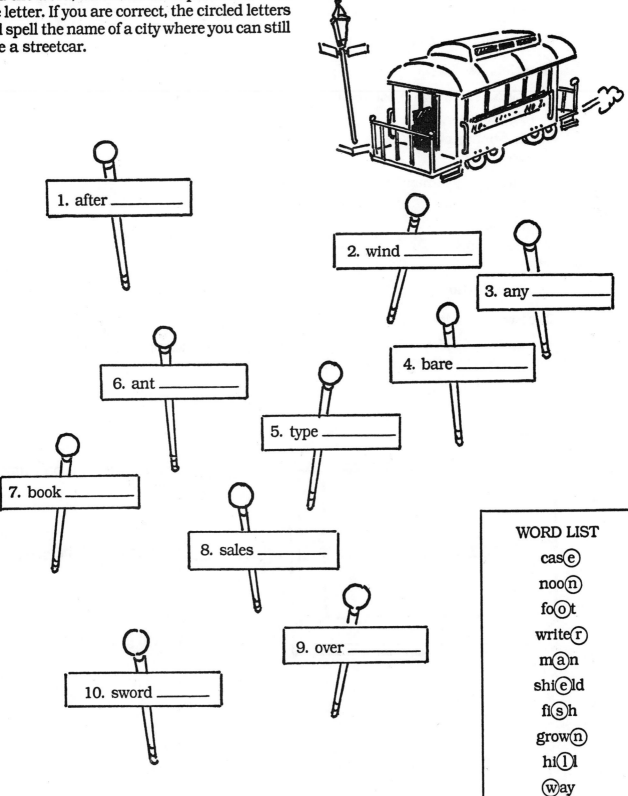

1. after _____

2. wind _____

3. any _____

4. bare _____

6. ant _____

5. type _____

7. book _____

8. sales _____

9. over _____

10. sword _____

WORD LIST

cas(e)

noo(n)

fo(o)t

write(r)

m(a)n

shi(e)ld

fi(s)h

grow(n)

hi(l)l

(w)ay

Bulletin Boards/Displays for Skill Reinforcement

The following bulletin boards and displays have been designed to provide the students with meaningful practice in using compound words.

Display Number One: Fly Away

Materials Needed:

blue heavyweight posterboard
green posterboard
felt-tipped pen
string
large plastic snap beads
glue
scissors
hole punch
tape
construction paper

Construction Directions:

1. This display will be placed in one section of shelves. The shelves will need to be spaced as shown here.

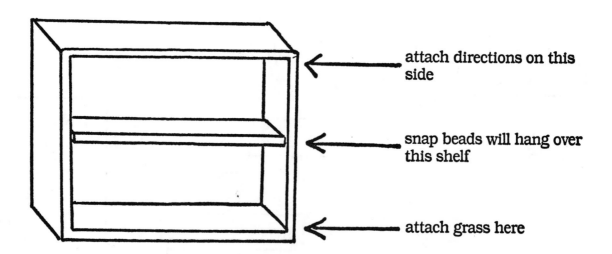

attach directions on this side

snap beads will hang over this shelf

attach grass here

2. Cut and mark the green posterboard using the grass pattern shown here. Tape it to the shelves as noted in the previous illustration.

3. Cut and mark the green posterboard using the tree directions pattern and tape it where noted on the shelf illustration.

4. Cut and mark the blue posterboard using the bird pattern shown here. You will need twelve.

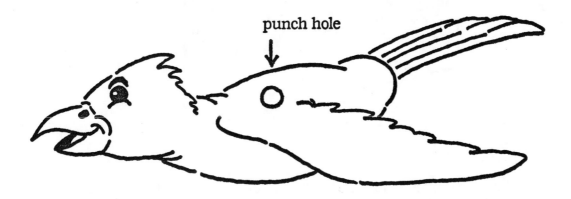

punch hole

5. Attach a long piece of string to one bird and then glue another bird to its back. This is to give it more weight. Now copy each of the following words on a different bird:

some, any, sail, blue, air, him

6. Fold a sheet of construction paper and print "Answer Key" on the front. Copy the following on the inside and attach to the tree trunk:

   something

   anyone

   sailboat

   bluebird

   airport

   himself

7. Thread the pieces of string behind and over the top shelf and attach a plastic snap bead to each. They will look something like the illustration below.

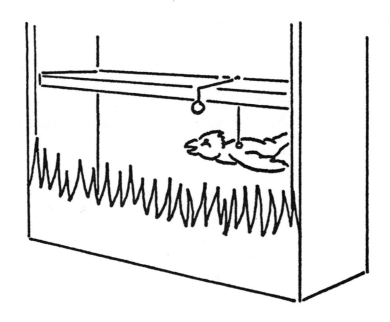

Display Use:

The children are to pull up the birds, one at a time, and determine which word on the tree trunk will form a compound word with the one on the bird. When they finish they may use the Answer Key.

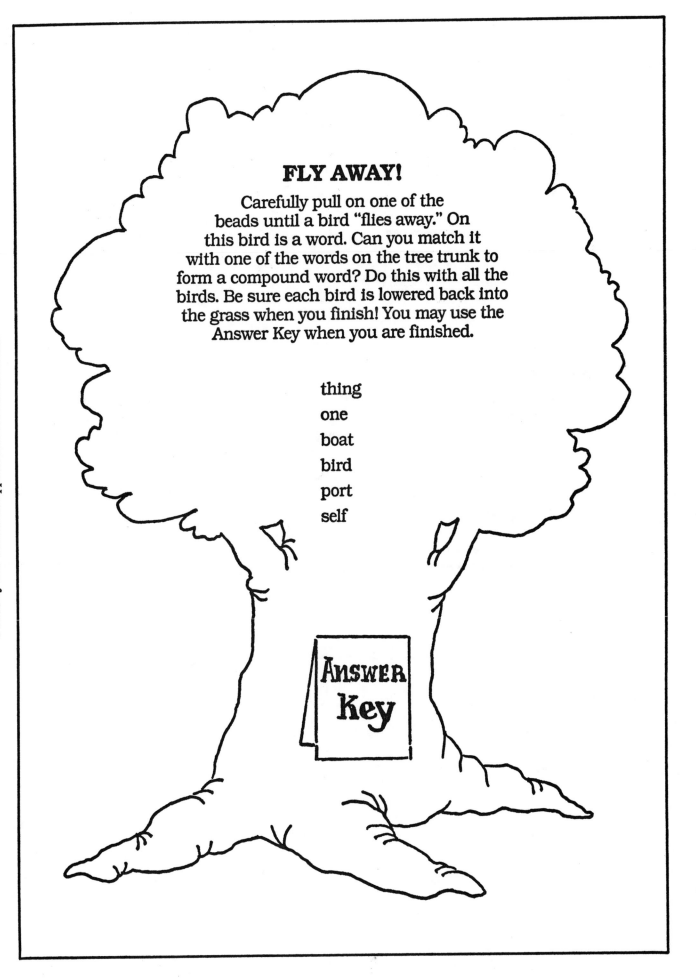

FLY AWAY!

Carefully pull on one of the beads until a bird "flies away." On this bird is a word. Can you match it with one of the words on the tree trunk to form a compound word? Do this with all the birds. Be sure each bird is lowered back into the grass when you finish! You may use the Answer Key when you are finished.

thing

one

boat

bird

port

self

ANSWER Key

Display Number Two: A Famous Flag

Materials Needed:

> blue background paper
> ditto box
> ditto paper
> white construction paper
> ditto master
> felt-tipped pens (various colors)
> tape
> scissors
> stapler

Construction Directions:

1. Use an opaque projector to trace the lettering and pirate ship on the background paper. Do not trace the masts or sails.
2. Cut the white construction paper to form sails and attach as shown in the illustration.

   NOTE: By stapling the ends closer together you will force the sails to bow outward from the board giving a three-dimensional effect.
3. Cut the ditto box in half across the width, cover with the white construction paper, print "Famous Flag Sheets" on the front, and attach it to the board.
4. Make copies of "A Famous Flag" activity sheet and place a supply in the bulletin board box.

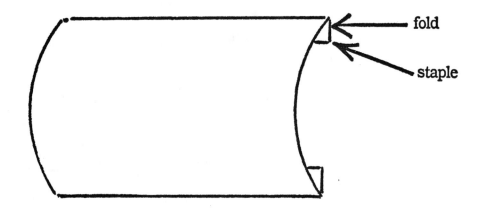

A FAMOUS FLAG

JOLLY ROGER

Directions:

1. What is the name of the flag on pirate ships?

2. Take one of the Famous Flag sheets and find out!

Famous Flag Sheets

Name _____

Date _____

What is the name of the flag on pirate ships?
In order to find out, copy the words in the
treasure chest next to those in the word list.
They each must form a compound word. Be
sure to circle the same letters that are circled
in the chest. If you are correct, the circled letters will spell the name of the pirate's flag.

life _____

after _____

ant _____

him _____

motor _____

when _____

with _____

some _____

book _____

air _____

Bulletin Board Use:

The children take an activity sheet and match the words in order to form compound words. If they fill in the sheet correctly, the circled letters will spell the name of the pirate's flag. (See the Answer Key.)

```
                    ANSWER KEY

     J   life(j)acket      R   wheneve(r)

     O   afterno(o)n       O   with(o)ut

     L   anthil(l)         G   somethin(g)

     L   himse(l)f         E   bookcas(e)

     Y   motorc(y)cle      R   airpo(r)t
```

Display Number Three: Compound Equations

Materials Needed:

white background paper
felt-tipped pens (various colors)
construction paper
stapler

Construction Directions:

1. Use an opaque projector to trace the lettering and figures onto the background paper.
2. Fold a sheet of construction paper and mark "Answer Key" on the front. Copy the following on the inside and attach to the board:

```
            ANSWER KEY

    1. fishhook    7. sundown

    2. rainbow     8. raincoat

    3. bedtime     9. hatbox

    4. starfish   10. houseboat

    5. pancake    11. bagpipe

    6. boxcar
```

COMPOUND EQUATIONS

Directions:

1. Number a sheet of paper from one to eleven.
2. Look at each "compound equation" and figure out the compound word.
3. Write the correct compound word next to each numeral.
4. Use the Answer Key when you are finished.

1.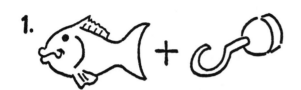

2.

3.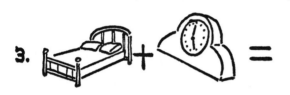

4.

5.

6.

7.

9.

8.

10.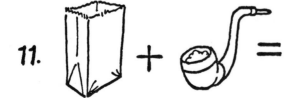

11.

Answer Key

Bulletin Board Use:

The children number a sheet of paper from one through eleven. They are to write down the compound word for each equation on the board. When they finish, they may use the Answer Key.

Display Number Four: Dr. Grimenstein . . . the Mad Scientist

Materials Needed:

background paper
posterboard
construction paper
felt-tipped pens (various colors)
long thumbtacks
small gelatin or pudding boxes
scissors
stapler
glue

Construction Directions:

1. Use an opaque projector to trace, mark, and cut the "mad scientist" from the posterboard. Attach the small gelatin boxes to the board and glue the "mad scientist" to these for a three-dimensional effect.

2. Cut and mark the posterboard using the flask pattern shown here. You will need seven.

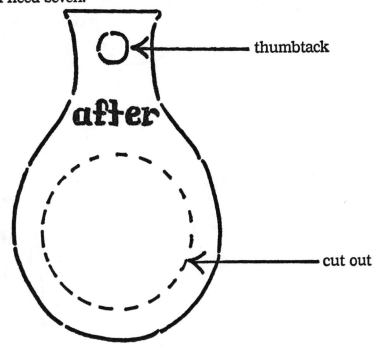

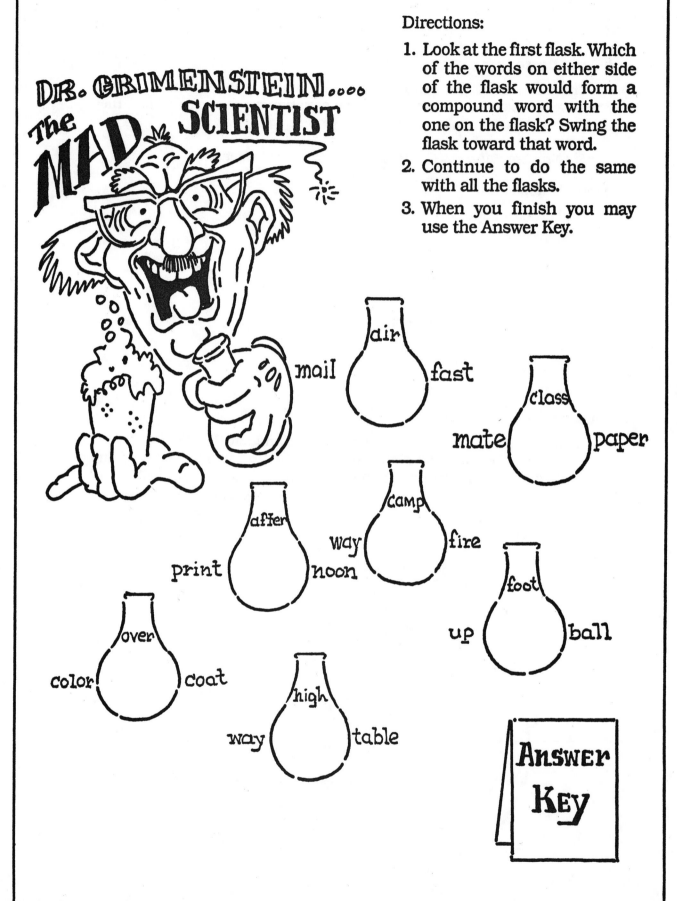

Directions:

1. Look at the first flask. Which of the words on either side of the flask would form a compound word with the one on the flask? Swing the flask toward that word.

2. Continue to do the same with all the flasks.

3. When you finish you may use the Answer Key.

3. Copy each of the following words on a different flask as shown in the illustration:

    after, air, class, camp, foot, high, over

4. Attach these to the board by using the thumbtack as shown in the pattern.

5. Use an opaque projector to finish tracing the lettering as shown in the illustration.

6. Fold a sheet of construction paper and mark "Answer Key" on the cover. Mark the following on the inside and attach to the board:

    airmail

    classmate

    afternoon

    campfire

    football

    overcoat

    highway

Bulletin Board Use:

The children look at the words on the flasks and decide which combine to form compound words. They do this by swinging the flasks toward the appropriate words. The correct word then shows through the cut-out portion of each flask. Students may use the Answer Key when they are finished.

SYNONYMS AND ANTONYMS

Introductory Lesson

Objective:

Children will be able to recognize the synonyms and antonyms of selected words.

Materials Needed:

chalkboard	paste
ditto master	posterboard
ditto paper	felt-tipped pen
magazines/catalogs	metal binder rings
scissors	

Introduction:

Tell the children they are going to make a class "Book of Crazy Definitions." Each one will be responsible for one page of the book. Copy the following on the chalkboard as you explain how the page is to be organized:

Each child will choose a word from the list you will copy on the chalkboard. (See Word List.) They will copy their word at the top of the paper and then look for a magazine picture that illustrates the opposite of that word. This picture should be pasted under the word and handed in to you. When you have received all of the sheets you should make a cover with the title "Book of Crazy Definitions" and bind the book with the metal rings.

IMPORTANT: Before having the children work independently at this project you should discuss picture ideas for a few of the words on the chalkboard. For example, a fire or stove for the word COLD, or an ant or baby for the word BIG.

WORD LIST				
poor	cold	new	small	work
fat	under	dry	mother	back
up	boy	low	open	old
hard	out	her	child	summer
late	stop	few	long	early
big	fast	dislike	day	short

Procedure:

Tell the children they are going to play a game. You will need to do the following to prepare for the game.

1. Print each of the following words on two sheets of white posterboard:

day	here	work	top	won
back	long	cool	hard	begin
summer	good	all	push	stand

2. Print each of the following words on two sheets of yellow posterboard:

night	there	play	bottom	lost
front	short	warm	soft	end
winter	bad	none	pull	sit

Now divide the class into two equal teams. Distribute one set of white word cards to each team. Be sure that every child has at least one card.

You will now hold up the yellow word cards one at a time in flashcard fashion. After a yellow card is held up, one child from each team must hold up a word that means the opposite. The first team to hold up the correct word card receives two points. The team with the most points at the end of the game is the winner.

> NOTE: If a child holds up the wrong word card, two points are deducted from the team's score. If a child holds up the correct word card, but another on the same team holds up a wrong card, one point is deducted from the team's score.

Evaluation:

Use the activity sheet "On Their Way Home" to see how well your students understand selected antonyms. Before distributing copies of the activity sheet, you should copy the following on the chalkboard or a transparency:

(1) tall   _____

(2) winter _____

(3) mother_____

(4) play   _____

(5) late   _____

(6) wet   _____

___ ___ ___ ___ ___ ___

WORD LIST

s(u)mmer

wor(k)

shor(t)

dr(y)

fathe(r)

(e)arly

Using the students' suggestions, fill in the blanks by finding words from the Word List that mean the opposite of those words in the first line. Have the students circle the letters that are circled in the Word List. When they are finished, they should copy down the circled letters on the blanks provided. If the students are correct, the circled letters will spell something many people eat for Thanksgiving dinner. (See the Answer Key.)

```
ANSWER KEY

T    shor(t)

U    s(u)mmer

R    fathe(r)

K    wor(k)

E    (e)arly

Y    dr(y)
```

When you think your students understand the procedure, distribute the activity sheet and let them begin. You should take note of those children having difficulty with this assignment and plan a special group session to reteach the selected antonyms.

The activity sheet is self-correcting. As shown in the answer key, the words DAPPER DAN will be spelled if the sheet is completed correctly.

```
ANSWER KEY

D    (d)ay

A    (a)ll

P    (p)ush

P    sto(p)

E    n(e)w

R    ha(r)d

D    (d)own

A    b(a)d

N    e(n)d
```

ON THEIR WAY HOME

© 1998 by The Center for Applied Research in Education

Name _____

Date _____

Josh and his pony are on their way home. You are to follow their path home. When you come to a word, you must find another word in the Word List that means the opposite. Write this word on the blank. Now continue along the path doing the same thing for each word. Be sure to circle the letters in the words that are circled in the Word List. When you are finished, copy the circled letters on the blanks at the bottom of this sheet. If you are correct, these letters will spell the name of Josh's pony.

3. pull

_____

2. none

_____

1. night

_____

4. go

_____

5. old

_____

7. up

_____

6. easy

_____

8. good

_____

9. begin

_____

WORD LIST

(p)ush

n(e)w

b(a)d

(d)ay

(a)ll

ha(r)d

e(n)d

(d)own

sto(p)

__ __ __ __ __ __ __ __ __

Bulletin Boards/Displays for Skill Reinforcement

The following bulletin boards and displays have been designed to provide the students with meaningful practice in synonym and antonym usage.

Display Number One: Ladybug, Ladybug, Fly Away Home!

Materials Needed:

white background paper
felt-tipped pens (various colors)
library-book card pockets
legal-size envelope
orange construction paper
orange tissue paper
10 strips of 2″ x 6″ posterboard
stapler

Construction Directions:

1. Use the opaque projector to trace the lettering and figures onto the background paper. Use the felt-tipped pens and color appropriately.

2. Cut the tissue paper using the following flame pattern and attach to the board around the house:

3. Attach the library-book card pockets to the board as shown in the illustration. Print one of the following words on each card pocket:

late	old	push	down	light
cold	run	tall	high	rich

LADYBUG, LADYBUG, FLY AWAY HOME!

Directions:

1. Take the word cards out of the holder.

2. Follow the ladybug's path. When you come to a word pocket, read the word. Now find a word on one of your cards that means the opposite of the word. Place it in the pocket. Continue this until you reach the burning home.

3. Use the Answer Key when you have finished to see how well you did.

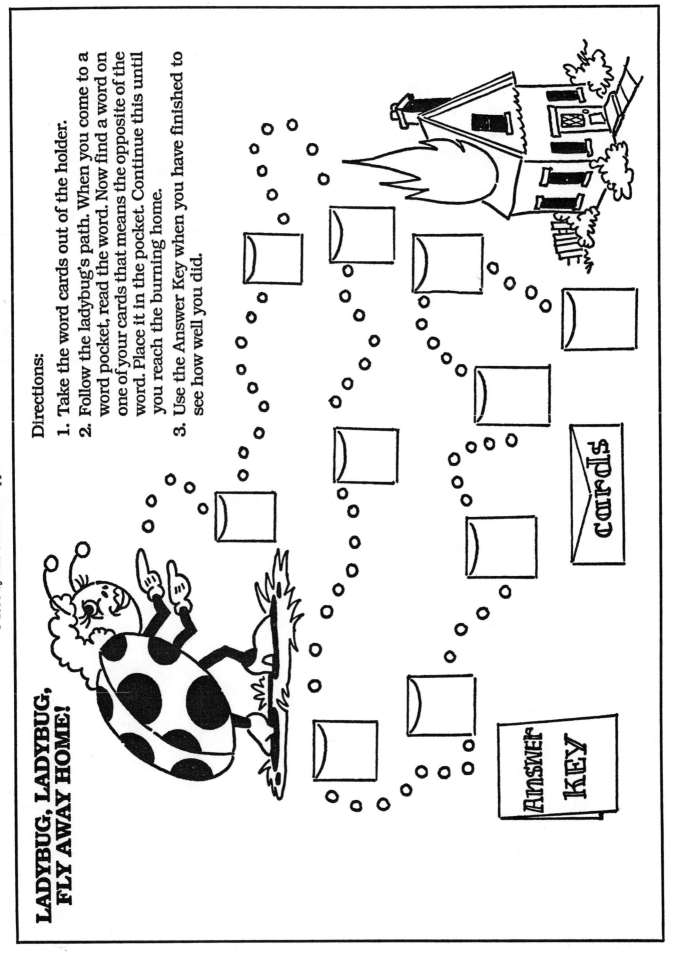

cards

Answer KEY

4. Print one of the following words on each of the posterboard strips:

early   new   pull   up   dark
poor   hot   walk   low   short

5. Fold the orange construction paper and mark "Answer Key" on the front. Copy the following on the inside and attach to the board:

late – early

light – dark

run – walk

old – new

rich – poor

tall – short

push – pull

cold – hot

high – low

down – up

6. Attach the large envelope to the board and place the word cards in it.

Bulletin Board Use:

Children take the word cards out of the envelope. Following the ladybug's path, they try to find an antonym for each word pocket. The children place the word cards in the correct pockets. When they finish, they may use the Answer Key.

Display Number Two: Andre's Antonyms

Materials Needed:

heavyweight white posterboard

felt-tipped pens (various colors)

large manila envelope

tape

glue

scissors

razor-blade knife

ditto master

ditto paper

Construction Directions:

1. Cut and mark the posterboard using an enlargement of the Andre pattern. The figure should be at least three feet in height.

Take one of my
activity sheets
and complete it.

ANDRE'S ANTONYMS

Name _____

Date _____

See if you can work Andre's puzzle. Look at the
first word in the Word List. Now look for a
word on one of the ants that means the opposite of this word and write it on the line. Be
sure to circle the letter that is circled. Do this
with all of the words. When you are finished,
copy the circled letters on the spaces at the
bottom of this page. If you are correct, the
circled letters will spell how well you did.

WORD LIST

scared _____

all _____

there _____

work _____

dark _____

lost _____

warm _____

up _____

___ ___ ___ ___ ___   ___ ___ ___ ___ ___

2. Cut a slit in the arm, as shown in the illustration, and slide the manila envelope through this slit. Tape the envelope to the backside of the figure.

3. Cut, fold, and tape a sheet of posterboard to the back of Andre using an enlargement of the pattern shown here. This will allow the figure to stand on a table or a shelving unit.

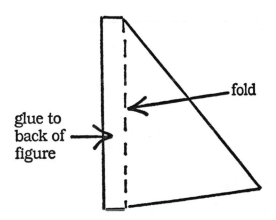

4. Duplicate the "Andre's Antonyms" activity sheet and place a supply in the envelope.

Display Use:

Children are to take an activity sheet and correctly match the antonym word pairs. The sheet is self-correcting. The words VERY GOOD will be spelled if it is correctly completed. (See the Answer Key.)

ANSWER KEY

V   bra(v)e

E   non(e)

R   he(r)e

Y   pla(y)

G   li(g)ht

O   w(o)n

O   co(o)l

D   (d)own

Display Number Three: From the Planet Gorgi

Materials Needed:

> white background paper
> white posterboard
> blue construction paper
> small gelatin or pudding boxes
> felt-tipped pens (various colors)
> stapler
> scissors
> legal-size envelope
> straight pins
> hole punch
> glue

Construction Directions:

1. Use an opaque projector to trace the figures and lettering onto the background paper. Use appropriate colors.
2. Use the opaque projector to trace the large title planet on the white posterboard. Attach the small gelatin boxes to the board and glue the planet to these for a three-dimensional effect.
3. Attach the straight pins over the clouds as shown in the illustration.
4. Cut, punch, and mark the white posterboard using the spaceship pattern shown here. You will need eight.

5. Print each of the following words on a different spaceship as shown in the illustration:
   STOP, HAVE, ONE, LOOK, LIKE, MAKE, NAME, LITTLE

Directions:

1. Take the spaceships out of the envelope.
2. Look at the word on one of the clouds. Can you find a word on a spaceship that means the same? If you can, hang it on the hook over that cloud. Do the same with all the spaceships.
3. You may use the Answer Key when you are finished.

own

single

see

small

halt

enjoy

title

build

FROM THE PLANET GORT

Spaceships

Answer Key

6. Mark "Spaceships" on the envelope, attach it to the board, and place all the spaceships in it.

7. Fold a sheet of blue construction paper and mark the front "Answer Key" as shown in the illustration. Print the following on the inside and attach it to the board:

stop – halt	like – enjoy
have – own	make – build
one – single	name – title
look – see	little – small

Bulletin Board Use:

The children take the spaceships out of the envelope and match the words on these pieces with their synonyms on the clouds. To do this they hang the spaceships on the hooks above the appropriate clouds. They may use the Answer Key when they are finished.

Display Number Four: Eloise Goes to the Circus

Materials Needed:

white background paper

white posterboard

red construction paper

legal-size envelope

10 library-book card pockets or small envelopes

felt-tipped pens (various colors)

scissors

stapler

Construction Directions:

1. Use an opaque projector to trace the lettering and figures onto the background paper.

2. Print the following words, each on a different book card pocket and attach to the board as shown in the illustration:

GOOD	PUSH
ALL	FAST
HIGH	WON
OLD	BEGIN
STAND	SOFT

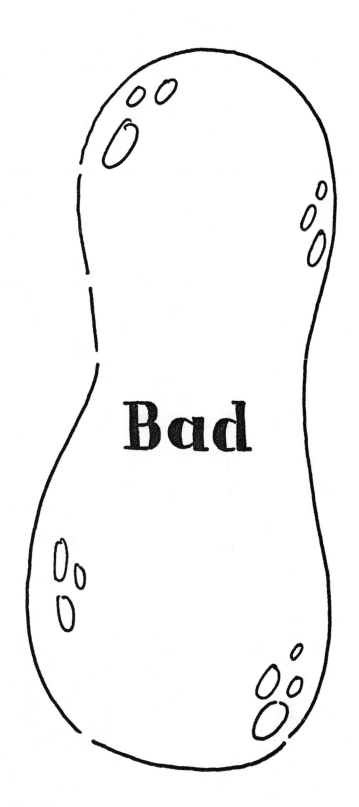

Bad

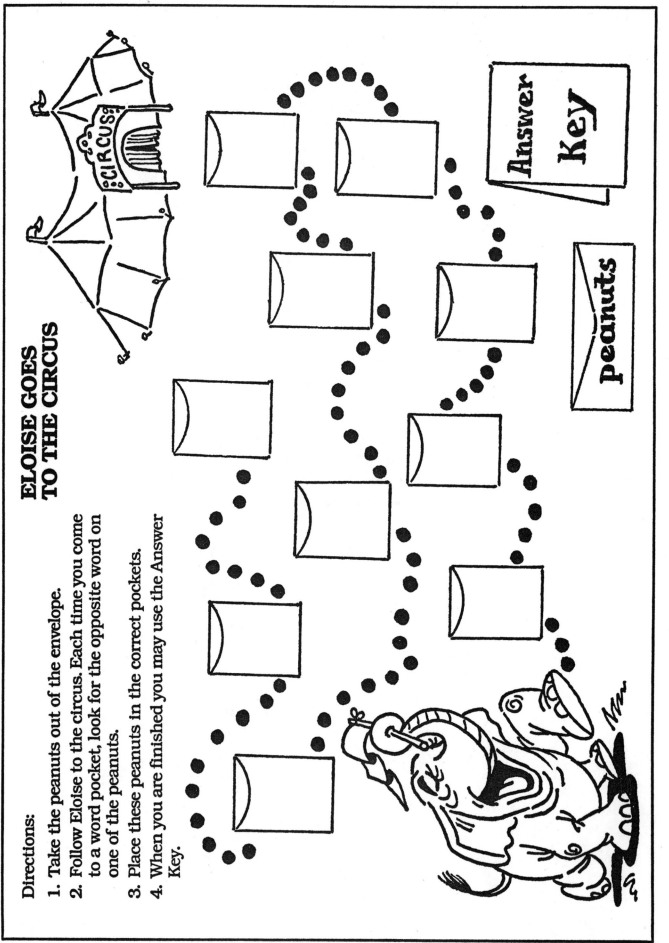

ELOISE GOES TO THE CIRCUS

Directions:

1. Take the peanuts out of the envelope.
2. Follow Eloise to the circus. Each time you come to a word pocket, look for the opposite word on one of the peanuts.
3. Place these peanuts in the correct pockets.
4. When you are finished you may use the Answer Key.

Answer Key

Peanuts

3. Cut and mark the white posterboard using the peanut pattern. Mark the following words, each on a different peanut:

BAD	NEW
NONE	LOW
PULL	LOST
SLOW	HARD
END	SIT

4. Mark "Peanuts" on the large envelope, attach it to the board, and place all the peanuts in it.

5. Fold a sheet of red construction paper and mark "Answer Key" on the cover. Copy the following on the inside and attach to the board:

good – bad	old – new
all – none	high – low
push – pull	won – lost
fast – slow	soft – hard
begin – end	stand – sit

Bulletin Board Use:

The children take the peanuts out of the envelope. Following the elephant's path, they try to find the antonym for each of the words listed on the pockets. They are to place the correct peanut in each pocket. They may use the Answer Key when they are finished.

CONTEXT CLUE USAGE

Introductory Lesson

Objective:

Children will be able to recognize selected words through the help of context clues.

Materials Needed:

chalkboard

ditto master

ditto paper

magazines/catalogs

scissors

paste

transparency

Introduction:

Tell the children that you went to a friend's house last night. Among other things you took a book to share with their children. After the children went to bed you and the friend had coffee and chatted for a while. When you were ready to leave for home you discovered that your friend's dog had chewed on the book.

NOTE: Please feel free to embellish this story in any manner you wish.

Now show them one of the pages from the book. Explain that you have made a transparency of the page so all could easily see. (See torn page.) Tell them that they can help you read this chewed page by filling in the missing words. Have the children take turns reading a line and filling in the missing word. (See Answer Key.)

```
ANSWER KEY

when, there, toward, he, found,

to, get, people, and, bag/box,

the, whistle, there, animals,

dressed, of, Johnny, good
```

Johnny was very excited _____

he went to the circus. _____

were many people walking _____

the main gate. Once _____

was inside the tent he _____

a seat that was as close _____

the center ring as he could _____

Before the circus began, several _____

came by selling balloons _____

candy. Johnny bought a _____

of popcorn from a lady. Then _____

ringmaster blew his _____

and the big parade began. _____

were all kinds of wild _____

in cages and circus people _____

in bright costumes. A group _____

clowns came out and made _____

laugh. He had a very _____

time at the circus!

Procedure:

Your students will need paper, pencils, scissors, paste, and magazines to complete this activity. After distributing the materials, write the following five sentences on a chalkboard or transparency:

We _____ around Grover's Lake yesterday.

Terry's new go-cart _____ down the street.

The _____ Ferris wheel spun faster and faster.

The ship _____ through the waves.

The _____ mansion sat on top of the hill.

Tell the students to copy the sentences and then look through magazines for three different words that can be used to fill in each sentence. The students are to cut out the words and paste them next to the appropriate sentences. Each student should find fifteen words.

When finished, have volunteers share their sentences orally so a comparison may be made.

Evaluation:

Use the activity sheet "Up the Tree" to see how well your students understand context clue usage.

Before distributing copies of the activity sheet, you should print the following onto a chalkboard or transparency:

I like to play _____.

How many stars can _____ see?

The _____ ran away from home.

____ ____ ____

```
+---------------------+
|     CLUE BOX        |
|     yo(u)           |
|     do(g)           |
|     (b)aseball      |
+---------------------+
```

Explain to the students that one word in each sentence is missing and may be found in the "Clue Box." Using the students' suggestions, copy the correct words into each sentence. Make sure you circle the letters that are circled in the box. When you are finished, copy down the circled letters on the spaces under the sentences. If the students were correct, these letters will spell something. (See the Answer Key.)

```
+---------------------+
|    ANSWER KEY       |
|    B  (b)aseball    |
|    U  yo(u)         |
|    G  do(g)         |
+---------------------+
```

Name _____

Date _____

How long do you think it will take the bug to climb up the tree? Read each sentence in the bug's path. A word is missing in each one, so look through the "Clue Box" to find the correct one. When you find it, write it on the space in the sentence. Be sure to circle the letter in each missing word and write the circled letters, starting with the letter closest to the bug, on the lines at the bottom of this page. If you are correct, the circled letters will spell how long it took the bug to climb up the tree.

UP THE TREE

We went there

_____.

We had _____
for dinner.

How far did you

_____?

Will _____ help me
with my homework?

_____ did you
buy that game?

The _____ was
filled with birds.

I _____ like to
go to the park.

How _____ will
we be leaving?

We stayed at the circus

_____ a long time.

CLUE BOX
ye(s)terday
fo(r)est
s(o)on
co(r)n
w(h)ere
y(o)u
(f)or
j(u)mp
wo(u)ld

_____ _____ _____ _____ _____ _____ _____ _____ _____

When you think your students understand the procedure, distribute the activity sheet and let them begin. You should take note of those children having difficulty with this assignment and plan a special group session to reteach context clue usage.

The activity sheet is self-correcting. As shown in the answer key, the words FOUR HOURS will be spelled if the sheet is completed correctly.

```
┌─────────────────────────────────┐
│          ANSWER KEY             │
│                                 │
│   F  (f)or        H  w(h)ere    │
│   O  s(o)on       O  y(o)u      │
│   U  wo(u)ld      U  j(u)mp     │
│   R  fo(r)est     R  co(r)n     │
│                   S  ye(s)terday│
│                                 │
└─────────────────────────────────┘
```

Bulletin Boards/Displays for Skill Reinforcement

The following bulletin boards and displays have been designed to provide the students with meaningful practice in context clue usage.

Display Number One: Poochie Pal

Materials Needed:

background paper
construction paper
felt-tipped pens (various colors)
stapler
scissors

Construction Directions:

1. Use an opaque projector to trace the figures and lettering onto the background paper.
2. Cut, mark, and fold the construction paper using the dog pattern shown here.

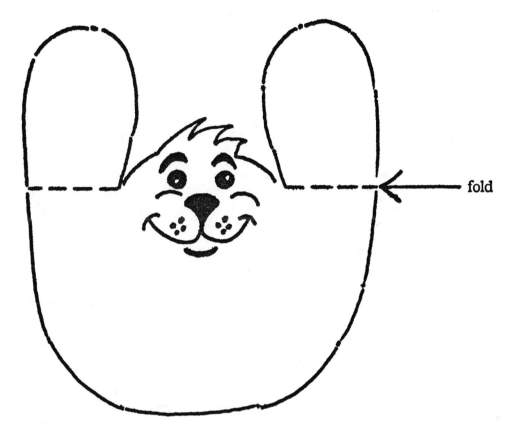

3. Mark each of the following on a different dog after the ears are folded as shown here. Mark "YES" and "NO" under the appropriate ears for the self-check:

I can't find my _____. (BONE, BIG)

I love to _____ holes. (DIG, BURY)

I _____ run fast. (LIKE, CAN)

I like _____ chase a stick. (SEE, TO)

I _____ flea powder. (NEED, WENT)

Who stepped on _____ tail? (IN, MY)

Where _____ my bowl? (IS, DOES)

4. Attach the dogs to the board as shown in the board illustration.

Directions:

1. Read the sentence on each dog.

2. Look at the words on the dog's ears. Which word do you think is the word missing in the sentence? When you think you know, lift the dog's ear to see if you are correct!

POOCHIE PAL

Bulletin Board Use:

The children are to read the sentence on each dog and find the missing word on one of the dog's ears. When they think they know, they flip up the appropriate ear for the self-check.

Display Number Two: WITCH Is Correct?

Materials Needed:

background paper	stapler
yellow posterboard	glue
tongue depressors	legal-size envelope
felt-tipped pens (various colors)	scissors
library-book card pockets	construction paper

Construction Directions:

1. Use an opaque projector to trace the lettering and figures onto the background paper.

2. Attach the library-book card pockets and write each of the following sentences on a different pocket:

The witch _____ flying on her broom.

The witch is _____ for her black cat.

The black cat is _____ .

The witch is going to _____ friend's house.

The witch is late and is in a _____ .

It is _____ dark outside.

3. Mark and cut the yellow posterboard into the following broom pattern. Use the tongue depressors for the broom handles. You will need six.

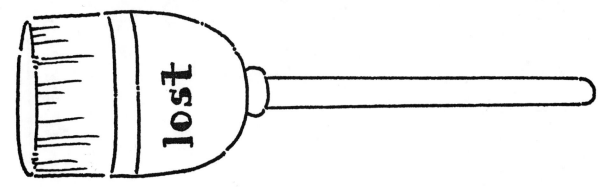

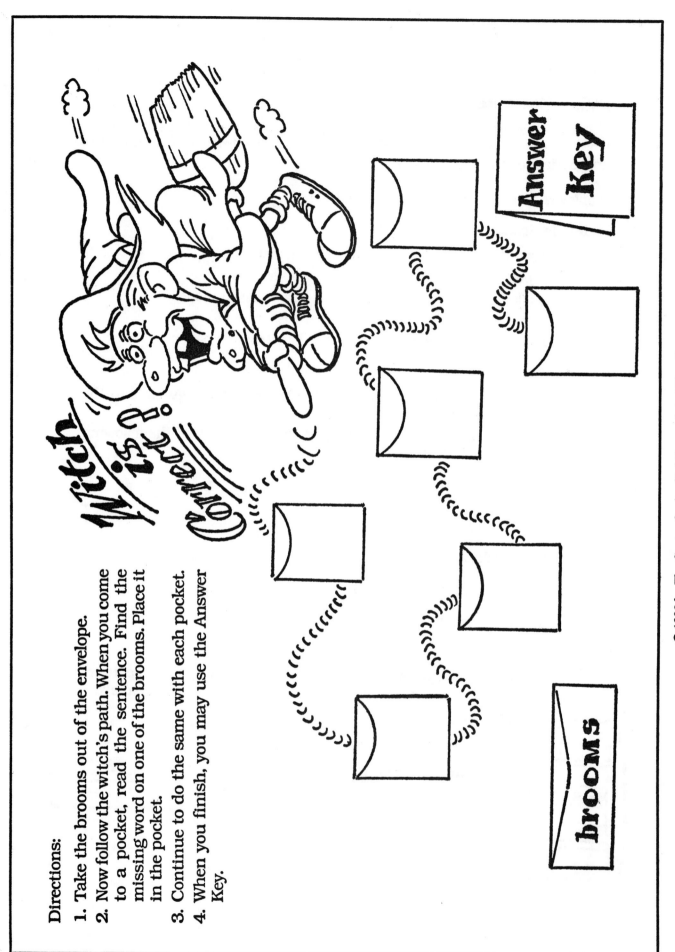

Directions:

1. Take the brooms out of the envelope.
2. Now follow the witch's path. When you come to a pocket, read the sentence. Find the missing word on one of the brooms. Place it in the pocket.
3. Continue to do the same with each pocket.
4. When you finish, you may use the Answer Key.

Witch Wis is Correct?

Answer Key

brooms

4. Print the following words, each on a different broom as shown in the illustration:

    is, looking, lost, her, hurry, very

5. Fold a sheet of construction paper and mark "Answer Key" on the cover. Copy the following on the inside and attach to the board:

    The witch IS flying on her broom.

    The witch is LOOKING for her black cat.

    The black cat is LOST.

    The witch is going to HER friend's house.

    The witch is late and is in a HURRY.

    It is VERY dark outside.

Bulletin Board Use:

The children take the brooms from the envelope and try to match the missing words on the brooms to the sentences on the pockets. They do this by placing the brooms in the pockets. When finished, they are to use the Answer Key.

Display Number Three: Whooo Did It?

Materials Needed:

background paper

small brown lunch bag

construction paper

newspaper

string

felt-tipped pens (various colors)

glue

stapler

scissors

ditto box

ditto master

ditto paper

Construction Directions:

1. Use an opaque projector to trace the lettering and figures onto the background paper.

2. Make the following owl using the paper bag, newspaper, string, construction paper, and felt-tipped pens. Then attach it to the board as shown in the board illustration.

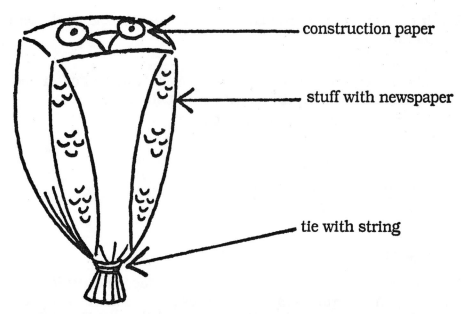

construction paper

stuff with newspaper

tie with string

3. Cut the ditto box in half across the width, cover with construction paper, print "Whooo Sheets" on the front, and attach it to the board.

4. Duplicate copies of the "Whooo" sheets and place a supply in the box.

Bulletin Board Use:

The children take an activity sheet and fill in the missing words in the sentences. If they fill in the sheet correctly, the circled letters will spell the words HIS DOG, ROVER. (See the Answer Key.)

ANSWER KEY

H   t(h)e

I   B(i)lly's

S   boy(s)

D   (d)og

O   n(o)t

G   (g)one

R   (r)an

O   every(o)ne

V   o(v)er

E   aft(e)r

R   dinne(r)

WHOOO DID IT?

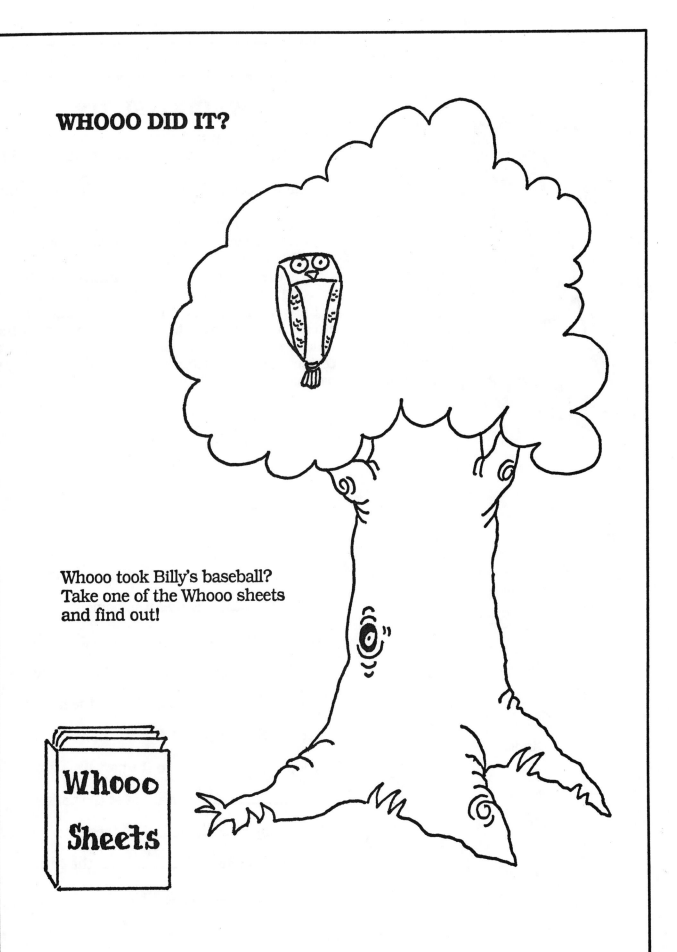

Whooo took Billy's baseball?
Take one of the Whooo sheets
and find out!

WHOOO DID IT?

"Hurry up!" yelled Tom.

"I will," answered Billy as he ran into his house.

Billy needed his baseball. The gang was waiting for him. He looked in his room but it wasn't there. It wasn't in the hall closet either.

"Now where could it be?" he wondered.

Well, where do you think it is?

Do the following puzzle and find out. Fill in the missing word in each sentence. You can find them in the word list. Be sure to circle the letters that are circled in the word list. Copy these letters on the spaces at the bottom of this sheet. If you are correct, the circled letters will spell who took Billy's baseball.

WORD LIST

every(o)ne
boy(s)
(r)an
aft(e)r
(d)og
dinne(r)
t(h)e
(g)one
n(o)t
o(v)er
B(i)lly's

_____ boys were going to play.

_____ mother was home.

Where would the _____ play ball?

Billy's _____ was wagging his tail.

Tom did _____ go into the house.

The baseball was _____.

They _____ to the park.

_____ was waiting at the park.

Tom jumped _____ the fence.

They went home _____ the game.

Dad had _____ waiting.

___ ___ ___ ___ ___ ___ ___ ___, ___ ___ ___ ___ ___ ___

Display Number Four: Vicious Volcano

Materials Needed:

>   white background paper
>   brown crepe paper
>   felt-tipped pens (various colors)
>   ditto box
>   ditto master
>   ditto paper
>   cotton batting
>   construction paper
>   stapler
>   glue

Construction Directions:

1. Use the opaque projector to trace the lettering and figures onto the background paper. Do not draw the volcano.

2. Make the volcano by crushing the crepe paper. Then open it at the bottom, trim to shape, and attach to the board. Add cotton smoke and draw the rest with the felt-tipped pens as shown in the illustration.

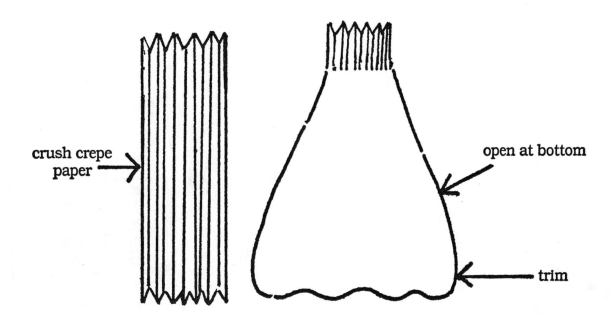

crush crepe paper →

open at bottom

trim

VICIOUS VOLCANO

Find out what volcano this is. Take an activity sheet and fill it in. If you are correct, you'll find out the name of this volcano.

Don't "blow your top"! Work one of the activity sheets.

Vicious Volcano Sheets

Name _____

Date _____

Read the sentences and fill in the missing words. You will find them in the volcano. Be sure to circle the letters that are circled in the words. When you finish, copy the circled letters on the spaces at the bottom of this page. If you are correct, these letters will spell the name of a famous volcano.

VICIOUS VOLCANO

_____ dog is missing.

Mother _____ us cookies.

We drove _____ the mountain.

Our _____ is filled with weeds.

If we don't hurry we'll be _____.

The teacher _____ out the window.

I _____ have enough money.

My _____ is coming to visit.

Ⓛooked

bⒶked

gardeⓃ

Ⓐunt

Ⓜy

lⒶte

Ⓤp

dⓄn't

___ ___ ___ ___ ___ ___   ___ ___ ___

3. Cut the ditto box in half across the width, cover with construction paper, print "Vicious Volcano Sheets" on the front, and attach to the board.

4. Make copies of the "Vicious Volcano" activity sheet and place a supply in the bulletin board box.

Bulletin Board Use:

The children take a puzzle sheet and fill in the missing words. If they are correct, the circled letters will spell the name of a volcano. (See the Answer Key.)

```
ANSWER KEY
M   (m)y
A   b(a)ked
U   (u)p
N   garde(n)
A   l(a)te

L   (l)ooked
O   d(o)n't
A   (a)unt
```

MAIN IDEAS

Introductory Lesson

Objective:

Children will be able to determine the main ideas of brief stories.

Materials Needed:

chalkboard
ditto master
ditto paper
transparency
tape
large cereal box
self-stick vinyl
crayons

Introduction:

Copy the following on a transparency:

(1) "It's raining!" shouted Bill. "Mom, may Sue and I put on our bathing suits and play in the rain?"

"Sure," answered his Mom. "Just dry off before you come back into the house."

(2) The rain kept falling. For two days Jane sat and watched it through her bedroom window. The street in front of her house was flooded, and she and her mom kept checking the house for leaks.

Never had it rained so much in her town in such a short time.

(3) "Oh, no," moaned Jim. "It has started to rain."

"Oh dear," said Sammy. "Now our baseball game will not be played!"

Print the following titles on the chalkboard:

Rain, Rain, Rain

The Ruined Day

Playing in the Rain

Tell the children to read the first story excerpt. Now have them read through the titles on the chalkboard deciding which is most appropriate for that story excerpt. (See the Answer Key.) Continue doing the same with the other two story excerpts.

```
ANSWER KEY

(1) Playing in the Rain

(2) Rain, Rain, Rain

(3) The Ruined Day
```

Procedure:

Read the following story to the children:

Aunt Bea's Ranch

Sue, Mark, and Bill were so excited that they could hardly stand it. It was thrilling enough to be going to visit their Aunt Bea out west on her ranch. But being able to ride the entire way on a train was almost more than they had ever hoped for. They all had enjoyed the ride and every so often would change seats so that everyone had a chance by the window. Mother and Father had put them on the train in Altanta, and Aunt Bea said that she would meet them at the Santa Fe train station.

As the train slowed and finally stopped at the Santa Fe station, all three children had their noses mashed against the window, each trying to see Aunt Bea first. Mark was the first to see her, and he gave out with a yelp! They grabbed their luggage and ran to greet her.

They put the luggage into the car and then climbed in themselves. Aunt Bea told them that her ranch was about an hour's drive from Santa Fe and that she had lunch ready and waiting. As they drove over the desert Aunt Bea explained to the children many of the things that they saw along the way. Sue was the first to see a giant cactus but Bill let out a yell when he spied a large rabbit. Aunt Bea told them that it was called an antelope jack rabbit. But mostly they just saw sand and more sand.

When they got to the ranch everyone was hungry and so they sat down under a large tree and had a picnic dinner. They were joined by Jake, Aunt Bea's hired hand. He told them that after they finished eating he would take them on a tour of the ranch in the jeep.

They were soon all piled into the little jeep with Jake at the steering wheel. The ride was so bumpy that they had to hang on so as not to fall off their seats. But Bill wasn't holding tight enough and slid right down on the floor. This made Mark laugh so hard that he lost his grip and ended up on the floor alongside his brother.

Jake showed them a beautiful lake on Aunt Bea's land where they would be allowed to swim and fish. He stopped the jeep and they all had a great time. They kicked off their shoes and went wading. They were all sorry that they had left their swimsuits back at the house. But Jake told them that he would bring them back the next day.

By the time they arrived back at the house the sun was setting. Aunt Bea had their beds turned down. All three children had a snack and went straight to bed. It had been a long day and they were all very tired. Besides, they had to rest for all that they planned to do the next day.

After you have finished reading the story, have the children think back through it. How did it begin? What was the first thing that happened? Where did it take place? Ask the children to think of all the various "scenes" in the story. List their suggestions on the chalkboard. Now tell each student to choose a scene and illustrate it.

Once they have finished, place the scenes in the correct story order and tape them together, end-on-end, to make a "film."

You will need to have made a "TV" by using a large cereal box. Simply cover with self-stick vinyl and then cut out an opening in the front and a slit in each side of the box.

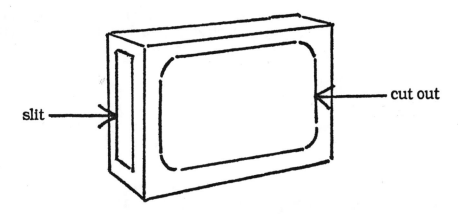

slit ——— ➤   ◄—— cut out

You are now ready to show the movie on TV! Just have the children slide the picture film through the slits in the box while you read the story. Be sure they change the picture each time a scene changes.

Evaluation:

Use the activity sheet "Whose Balloon?" to see how well your students can determine main ideas.

Before you distribute the activity sheet, you should read the following passage to your class:

It was Tony's turn at bat, and it was a good thing that Tony could hit because the Pirates were behind by two runs. All the kids cheered as Tony walked to the batter's box, but Tony wasn't smiling. He knew it was up to him to bring in the two players who were already on second and third bases. If he could do it, the score would be tied.

"Hit another home run, Tony!" yelled someone in the stands. Tony's batting average was good, and he had slammed a home run his last time at bat.

"Oh, if I can only connect with that ball now," he said.

Now ask the class to suggest a good title for the passage. List the students' ideas on the chalkboard and have them discuss the titles that best describe the central idea of the passage.

> VARIATION: If your students have difficulty suggesting titles, you might aid them by listing the following three titles and asking students to discuss them:
>
> The Home Run
>
> The Baseball Game
>
> Pressure on Tony

When you think your students understand the procedure, distribute the activity sheet and let them begin. You should take note of those children having difficulty with this assignment and plan a special group session to reteach main ideas.

WHOSE BALLOON?

Below are three stories, each in a hand. Read each story and draw a string from the hand to the balloon that shows the correct title for the story.

A Walk Through the Forest

Playing in the Forest

Lunch in the Forest

(1)
The forest was filled with the sound of birds and insects. Julie walked by some oak trees and heard the chattering of squirrels. The sun shone on the grass and flowers. Julie picked a few of these to take home.

(2)
"What did you bring?" asked Sally. She and Mary were having a picnic in the forest.
"I have sandwiches and cookies," answered Mary.
"Oh, good," said Sally. "I brought fruit and milk."
The two girls stopped at their favorite picnic spot near the creek and ate their lunch.

(3)
"Bet you can't find me!" yelled George. He and his friends were playing in the forest. It was George's turn to hide and he had found a place he was sure no one would look. It was in an old hollow log.

The activity sheet is easily corrected. Simply see that the following title/ story matches are made:

(1) A Walk Through the Forest

(2) Lunch in the Forest

(3) Playing in the Forest

Bulletin Boards/Displays for Skill Reinforcement

The following bulletin boards and displays have been designed to provide the students with meaningful practice in understanding main ideas.

Display Number One: The Spider's Web

Materials Needed:

background paper

black yarn

straight pins

posterboard

stapler

felt-tipped pens (various colors)

construction paper

legal-size envelope

black pipe cleaners

tape

hole punch

Construction Directions:

1. Use an opaque projector to trace the lettering and figures onto the background paper.

2. Attach the black yarn to form the web as shown in the illustration.

3. Print the following stories on the board as designated in the illustration:

Story One:

The spider walked to the edge of her web. She had not seen her children all day. After calling for them she returned to her home.

Story Two:

The spider's children were playing "king of the web." They were all yelling. The spider could not stand all the noise. She called for them to quiet down.

Story Three:

The spider was cooking in her kitchen. Her children could smell all kinds of good things. It was starting to get dark outside. The spider called for her children to come inside and wash up.

Story Four:

The spider and her children were walking to the pond. It had been a long time since they had been there. The children were jumping around they were so excited.

4. Cut, mark, and attach pipe cleaners to the posterboard using the spider pattern shown here. You will need four.

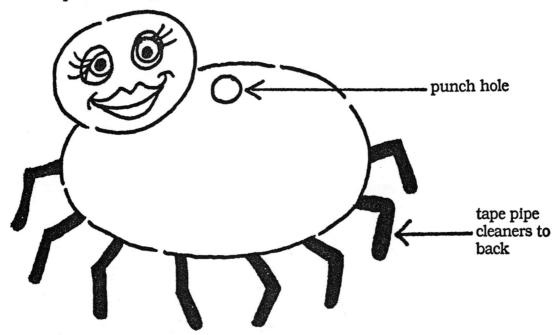

punch hole

tape pipe cleaners to back

5. Print the following titles, each on a different spider:

A Worried Spider

A Noisy Game

Dinner Time

Going Swimming

6. Mark "spiders" on the envelope, attach to the board and place the spiders in it.

7. Fold a sheet of construction paper and mark "Answer Key" on the front. Copy the following on the inside and attach it to the board:

(1) A Worried Spider

(2) A Noisy Game

(3) Dinner Time

(4) Going Swimming

THE SPIDER'S WEB

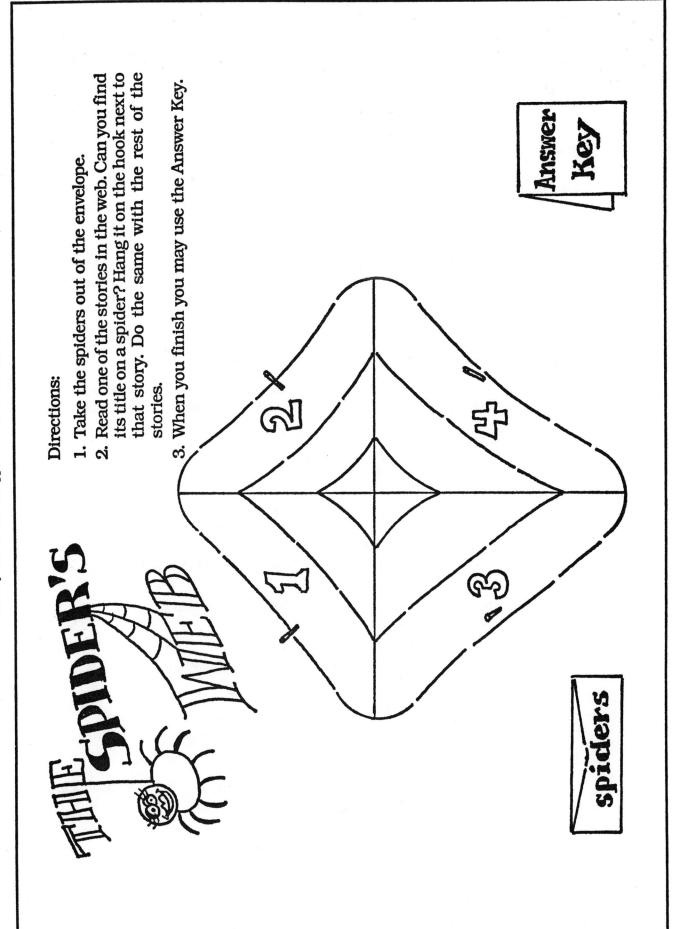

Directions:

1. Take the spiders out of the envelope.
2. Read one of the stories in the web. Can you find its title on a spider? Hang it on the hook next to that story. Do the same with the rest of the stories.
3. When you finish you may use the Answer Key.

Answer Key

spiders

2 1 4 3

Bulletin Board Use:

The children match the titles on the spiders with the stories in the web. They do this by hanging the spiders on the hooks next to the appropriate stories. They may use the Answer Key when finished.

Display Number Two: Circus Parade Mobile

Materials Needed:

posterboard
felt-tipped pens (various colors)
scissors
hole punch
string

Construction Directions:

1. Cut and mark the posterboard using an enlargement of the mobile pattern shown here. Attach these pieces together with string as shown.

2. Copy the following story on the circus tent:

   I bought a balloon at the circus from a man who must have been holding about twenty balloons. It was really difficult to choose which balloon to keep since he had so many different ones. There were yellow and green round balloons and blue ones that were long and narrow. One of the yellow round balloons had a cat's face painted on it. But the ones I liked best were the red balloons. They each were painted to look like clown faces. Some were happy and others were sad. I bought a happy one!

3. Copy each of the following titles on both sides of a different mobile piece:

   The Circus Balloons
   The Man at the Circus
   I Had Fun at the Circus
   The Clown Balloons
   The Circus Parade

Display Use:

The children are to read the story on the circus tent and then decide which of the story titles is the most appropriate. (The Circus Balloons)

Display Number Three: Unlock the Doors

Materials Needed:

background paper
felt-tipped pens (various colors)
construction paper
posterboard
pictures from basal readers
legal-size envelope
library-book card pockets
scissors
glue
stapler

Construction Directions:

1. Use an opaque projector to trace the lettering and figures onto the background paper.
2. Mount the pictures on the top halves of the doors and mark doorknobs as shown in the board illustration. Space the doors around the bulletin board.
3. Attach a library-book card pocket under each door and print a different numeral on each.
4. Cut and mark the posterboard using an enlargement of the following key pattern:

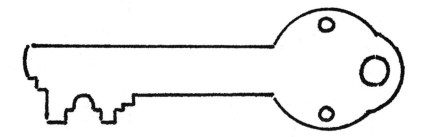

5. Print a title for each picture on a different key.
6. Print "Keys" on the envelope, attach to the board, and place the keys in it.
7. Fold a sheet of construction paper and print "Answer Key" on the cover. Copy the picture titles next to their appropriate numerals on the inside and attach it to the board.

Directions:

1. Take the keys out of the envelope.
2. Read the sentence on one of the keys. Can you find a door with the picture it describes? Place the key in the pocket under that door.
3. Do the same with the other keys.
4. Use the Answer Key when you finish.

Bulletin Board Use:

The children take the keys out of the envelope. They attempt to match each title with the picture it describes. They do this by placing the title key in the pocket under the appropriate picture. They may use the Answer Key when they finish.

Display Number Four: The Main Idea Niche

Materials Needed:

large cardboard box	legal-size envelope
construction paper	small pillow
self-stick vinyl or spray paint	glue
posterboard	stapler
pictures	scissors
library-book card pockets	felt-tipped pens (various colors)

Construction Directions:

1. Cover a large cardboard box (big enough for one child to sit in) with self-stick vinyl or use spray paint. If you use the paint plan on giving the box several light coats.

2. Cut and mark the posterboard using the following pattern and attach it to the wall behind the cardboard box:

3. Cut out pictures from old basal readers or magazines and mount them on the inside of the niche. Next to each picture attach a card pocket and print numerals on them.

4. Print a sentence describing one of the pictures on a strip of poster-board. Do this for all the pictures.

5. Mark the word "sentences" on the large envelope, attach it to a wall, and place the sentence strips in it.

6. Copy the following on the construction paper and attach it to a wall in the niche:

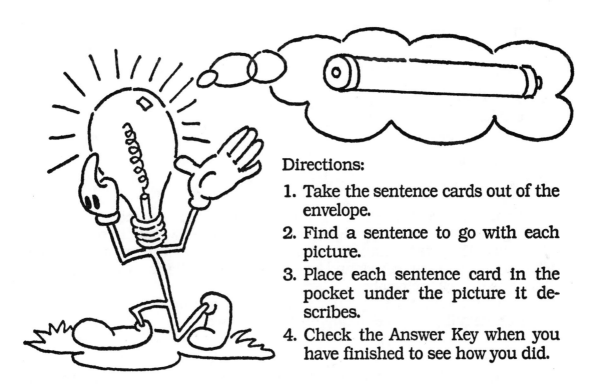

Directions:

1. Take the sentence cards out of the envelope.
2. Find a sentence to go with each picture.
3. Place each sentence card in the pocket under the picture it describes.
4. Check the Answer Key when you have finished to see how you did.

7. Fold a sheet of construction paper and mark "Answer Key" on the cover. Copy the sentences next to the correct numeral on the inside of the Answer Key and attach it to one of the inside walls of the box.

Display Use:

Children take the sentence strips out of the envelope and attempt to match each sentence with the picture it describes. When they think they know the answer, they place the sentence strips in the pockets under the appropriate picture. When they are finished, they use the Answer Key to check themselves.

IMPORTANT DETAILS

Introductory Lesson

Objective:

Children will be able to recognize important details in brief stories.

Materials Needed:

magazines/catalogs
scissors
paste
posterboard
chalkboard
ditto master
ditto paper

Introduction:

Construct a collage by cutting out many different magazine pictures and pasting them on a sheet of posterboard. Now show the children the collage for a short time. They are to remember as many of the things as they can. After the allotted time, cover the collage and have the children write down as many of the things as they can remember.

Using the students' suggestions, copy these items on the chalkboard. Now uncover the collage and see if anything was missed.

Procedure:

Read the following story aloud to the children:

"Boy . . . we turned on the television just in time," said Bill.

His sister, Amy, agreed. "The parade is just beginning. Look at the band. It sure is good. It must have over one-hundred marchers."

"Look what's next! What a great float . . . how do you suppose they made the palm tree and tropical flower garden look so real?" asked Bill. "It certainly must have taken them a long time to build."

"Aw . . . you like it because of the pretty ladies on it," teased Amy.

Bill ignored her remark because of the next thing in the parade. It was a huge balloon held down by long ropes that were anchored by men walking in the parade.

"Is that balloon a mouse or a bear?" asked Amy.

"It's a balloon of Smokey the Bear," answered Bill. "Look . . . here comes another large band."

"Yes, and look at the red and white cowboy uniforms they have. They must be a band from out west. See the bass drum . . . it says Oklahoma. Wow . . . they're a long way from home."

"Oh good, here come the clown cars," said Bill. "They're my favorite every year! Gee, there must be at least a dozen clowns riding all over them."

"Look at that one with the big red nose that lights up every time the car stops," laughed Amy.

"Here comes another balloon. Oh my gosh! It's a huge dragon. Doesn't he look mean?"

"I'm glad that he's just a balloon," said Amy. "But look at those beautiful horses coming next. I bet those riders are proud to be in the parade."

"Oh . . . here comes the first-place winning float. Isn't it beautiful?" sighed Amy. "It looks like those pictures of Switzerland in our geography books."

"Here comes another band . . . now what happened to the television? Try turning the brightness knob, Amy."

"It just won't come back on. Oh darn it, we'll miss the rest of the parade."

"I know," said Bill. "Let's run over to Jim's house. I'm sure he is watching it."

And so Bill and Amy did just that.

Now tell the children you are going to reread the story. But this time you will make certain changes in the story. They are to listen very carefully and write down as many of the changes as they can.

"Boy . . . we turned on the television just in time," said Bill.

His sister, Amy, agreed. "The parade is just beginning. Look at the band. It sure is good. It must have over fifty marchers."

"Look what's next! What a great float . . . how do you suppose they made that pine tree and tropical waterfall look so real?" asked Bill. "It certainly must have taken them a long time to build."

"Aw . . . you like it because of the pretty ladies on it," teased Amy.

Bill ignored her remark because of the next thing in the parade. It was a huge balloon held down by long ropes that were anchored by men walking in the parade.

"Is that balloon a mouse or a bear?" asked Amy.

"It's a balloon of Mickey Mouse," answered Bill. "Look . . . here comes another large band."

"Yes, and look at the red and white cowboy uniforms they have. They must be a band from out west. See the bass drum . . . it says New Mexico. Wow . . . they're a long way from home."

"Oh good, here come the clown cars," said Bill. "They're my favorite every year! Gee, there must be at least six clowns riding all over them."

"Look at that one with the big red ears that light up every time the car stops," laughed Amy.

"Here comes another balloon. Oh my gosh! It's a huge devil. Doesn't he look mean?"

"I'm glad that he's just a balloon," said Amy. "But look at those beautiful horses coming next. I bet those riders are proud to be in the parade."

"Oh . . . here comes the first-place winning float. Isn't it beautiful?" sighed Amy. "It looks like those pictures of Greece in our geography books."

"Here comes another band. Now what happened to the television? Try turning the vertical hold, Amy."

"It just won't come back on. Oh darn it . . . we'll miss the rest of the parade."
"I know," said Bill. "Let's run over to Jim's house. I'm sure he is watching it."
And so Bill and Amy did just that.

Using the students' suggestions, write the changes on the chalkboard.
Compare their list with the list in the Answer Key.

```
┌─────────────────────────────────────────────┐
│              ANSWER KEY                      │
│   one-hundred - - - - fifty                  │
│           palm - - - - pine                  │
│   flower garden - - - - waterfall            │
│ Smokey the Bear - - -   Mickey Mouse         │
│       Oklahoma - - - - New Mexico            │
│       a dozen - - - - six                    │
│           nose - - - - ears                  │
│         dragon - - -  devil                  │
│   Switzerland - - - - Greece                 │
│ brightness knob - - - - vertical hold        │
└─────────────────────────────────────────────┘
```

Evaluation:

Use the activity sheet "At the Circus" to see how well your students
remember details.

Before distributing the activity sheet, read the following story to your
students:

The Playground

We had fun on the new playground yesterday. There were five swings near the
back of the playground. They were really big so you could swing high.

On the other side of the playground were a merry-go-round and two slides. One
slide was smaller than the other.

A seesaw was in the center of the playground. I hope to go back to the playground
today and play some more.

When you finish reading the story, have the children draw the playground
on a sheet of paper. After they have completed their drawings, read the following list of playground details so they may correct their own papers:

–five tall swings near the back of the playground

–one merry-go-round next to the two slides on the other side of the play-ground

–one slide smaller than the other

–one seesaw in the center of the playground

When you think your students understand the procedure, distribute copies of the activity sheet and let them begin. You should take note of those children having difficulty with this assignment and plan a special group session to reteach story details.

When evaluating the students' activity sheets, it is important to remember that the various students' drawings might look different and still be correct. The important thing is that all the details have been included in the drawings, as shown in the Answer Key here.

ANSWER KEY

Name _____

Date _____

AT THE CIRCUS

I saw five dogs doing tricks at the circus. They were white with black spots. Two of them were jumping through hoops. Two more were sitting on their hind legs and balancing blue balls on their noses. The fifth dog sat in a chair pretending to read a newspaper. I really liked the dogs and wish I could have taken them home with me!

Bulletin Boards/Displays for Skill Reinforcement

The following bulletin boards and displays have been designed to provide the students with meaningful practice in determining important details.

Display Number One: Bertrum Bunny

Materials Needed:

background paper
two bottom halves of cereal boxes
construction paper
posterboard
felt-tipped pens (various colors)
stapler
scissors
tape

Construction Directions:

1. Use the opaque projector to trace the lettering and the figures in the bulletin board illustration on the background paper. Use the felt-tipped pens.
2. Cover the bottom halves of the cereal boxes with brown construction paper, and attach two strips of brown construction paper for handles. Label each as shown in the illustration. Attach the baskets and the labels to the board.
3. Cut and mark the white posterboard pieces in the egg shape shown here. You will need eight.

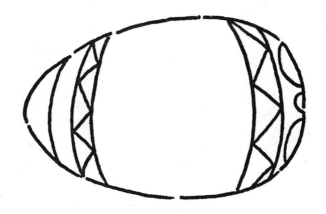

4. Print each of the following paragraphs on a different egg:

(A) Bertrum has been hiding Easter eggs. He has hidden three under the bush and two near the tree. He must hurry before the children arrive.

(B) Bertrum has been hiding Easter eggs. He has just begun and so has hidden only one. It is near the tree. He must hurry before the children arrive.

(C) Bertrum has been hiding Easter eggs. He has hidden five in the grass and two under the bush. He is hurrying before the children arrive.

(D) Bertrum has been hiding Easter eggs. He has just hidden three in the tall grass and one next to the tree. He must hurry before the children arrive.

5. Copy the following drawings, each on a different egg:

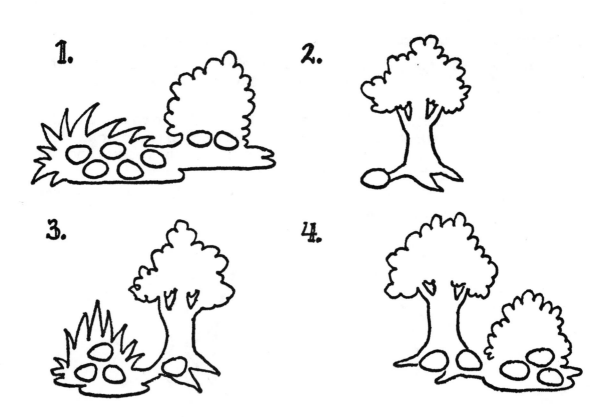

1.

2.

3.

4.

BERTRUM BUNNY

Help me fill up my baskets with eggs! Follow the directions in the large egg.

1. Take the eggs out of the baskets.

2. Read one of the story eggs and look for the picture egg it describes.

3. Do this with all the eggs.

4. Use the Answer Key when you are finished.

Answer Key

6. Place the "picture eggs" in one basket and the "story eggs" in the other.
7. Fold the sheet of construction paper, mark "Answer Key" on the cover and the inside as shown below, and attach it to the board:

    A – 4
    B – 2
    C – 1
    D – 3

Bulletin Board Use:

The children are to take the eggs out of the baskets. They are to match the "story eggs" with their "picture eggs." When they finish, they are to use the Answer Key.

Display Number Two: A DEVIL of a Time!

Materials Needed:

large cardboard box	posterboard
self-stick vinyl	scissors
razor-blade knife	tape
felt-tipped pens (various colors)	glue
construction paper	long shoelaces

Construction Directions:

1. Cut the cardboard box in half, from one corner to the opposite corner as shown here. Cover it with self-stick vinyl.

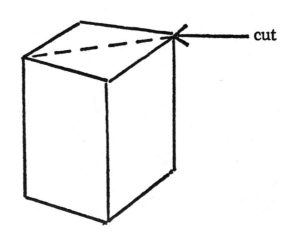

2. Cut and mark the posterboard using the devil pattern shown here. Attach it to the wall above the display.

3. Print each sentence on a piece of construction paper and attach to the top of the display. Attach a long shoelace next to each sentence as shown in the illustration. Be sure to copy the letters next to the cards:

   A. The Devil jumped over the river and ran into the woods.
   B. The Devil rushed around the tree and hopped over the fence.
   C. The Devil ran across the street and hid behind the car.
   D. The Devil ran out of the house and into the car.

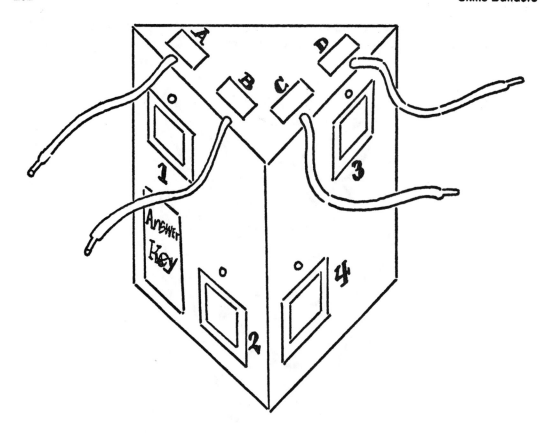

4. Use an opaque projector to copy the following "devil drawings" onto sheets of drawing paper and attach to the display:

1.

2.

3.

4.

5. Use the construction paper to make frames for these drawings as shown here.

a.

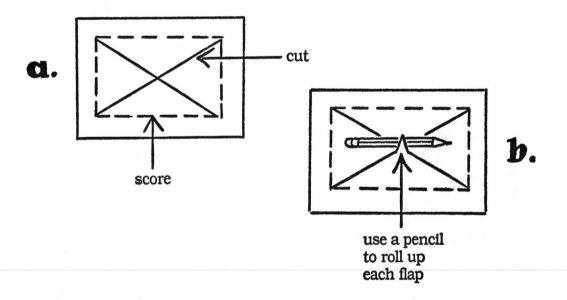

cut

score

b.

use a pencil
to roll up
each flap

c.

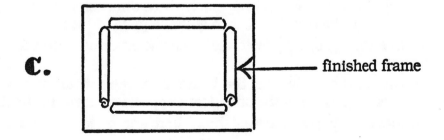

finished frame

6. Attach one of these frames over each of the drawings and punch a hole next to each.

7. Fold a sheet of construction paper and mark Answer Key on the cover. Copy the following on the inside and attach to the display:

    A – 4

    B – 1

    C – 3

    D – 2

Display Use:

The children are to match the sentences with their pictures by placing the shoelaces into the correct holes. When finished, they may use the Answer Key.

Display Number Three: Cupboard Confusion

Materials Needed:

    white background paper

    felt-tipped pens (various colors)

    construction paper

    scissors

    stapler

    glue

    small gelatin or pudding boxes

    posterboard

    plain paper plates

    long thumbtacks

    string

    small lightweight boards to use as shelving

Construction Directions:

1. Use an opaque projector to trace the lettering and plate onto the posterboard. Cut out the plate and attach it to the board with the small gelatin boxes as backing for a three-dimensional effect. Staple the boxes to the board and then glue the plate to these.

2. Use the opaque projector to trace the lettering onto the background paper.

3. Attach the shelves to the board by placing thumbtacks under the shelves and using the string for support as shown in the illustration.

4. Mark the paper plates as shown here and place on the bottom shelf.

CUPBOARD CONFUSION

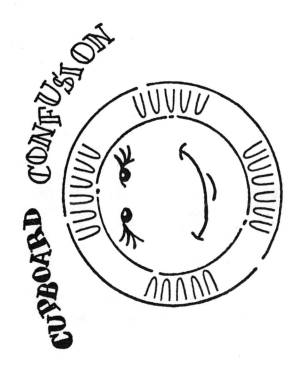

Directions:

1. Take a sentence plate off the bottom shelf. Read it.

2. Look through the picture plates to find the matching one. Place these together on the top shelf.

3. Do this with all of the plates. You may use the Answer Key when you finish.

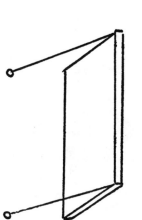

Answer Key

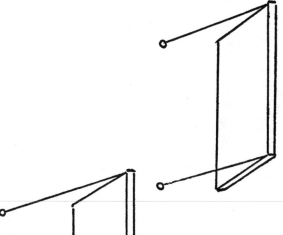

5. Print the following sentences, each on a different paper plate:

   The dog is in its house.

   The dog has a bone.

   The dog is running after the cat.

   The dog and cat are friends.

   The dog is sitting on its house.

   The dog is jumping over the bone.

   The dog can't find the bone.

6. Tape two pieces of construction paper together along one side and mark "Answer Key" on the top piece. Make a reduction of each picture plate with the correct sentence written on it and glue these inside the Answer Key. Attach to board.

Bulletin Board Use:

The children are to match the sentence plates with their correct picture plates and place them on the top shelf. When finished, they may use the Answer Key.

Display Number Four: Snowy Cove

Materials Needed:

- large cardboard box
- white construction paper
- felt-tipped pens (various colors)
- library-book card pockets
- glue
- tape
- stapler
- razor-blade knife
- scissors
- posterboard
- white corrugated paper
- white straws
- straight pins

Construction Directions:

1. Cut the front off the large box.

2. Cut the white corrugated paper into an icicle pattern and attach to the top front of the box as shown in the illustration.

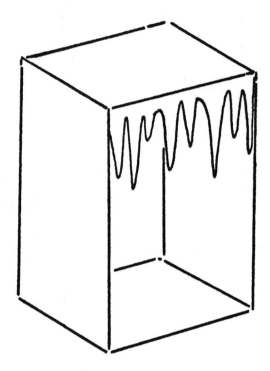

3. Cut out large snowballs from the construction paper. Copy each of the following drawings on a different snowball and attach a library-book card pocket next to each snowball. Attach these to the interior walls of the box.

4. Print each of the following sentences on a different strip of posterboard:

It was snowing on the snowman.

The snowman smiled at the children.

The snowman was melting.

A child put a hat on the snowman.

The snowman fell over.

A rabbit looked at the snowman.

5. Attach a card pocket on an inside wall and place the sentence strips in it.

6. Copy the following directions on a large snowball and attach to a wall:

Directions:

1. Take the sentence cards out of the pocket.
2. Read one of the sentences. Find the picture and place the card in that pocket.
3. Do the same with all the sentence cards.
4. You may use the Answer Key when you finish.

7. Fold a sheet of construction paper and mark "Answer Key" on the front. Copy the following on the inside:

    1 – It was snowing on the snowman.
    2 – The snowman smiled at the children.
    3 – The snowman was melting.
    4 – The child put a hat on the snowman.
    5 – The snowman fell over.
    6 – A rabbit looked at the snowman.

8. Make the following straw snowflakes and attach to the inside walls with straight pins:

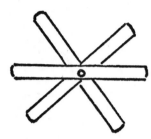

Cut each straw into three parts and push pin through the midde.

Display Use:

The children read the sentence strips and match them with their appropriate pictures. They do this by placing each strip in the pocket beneath the picture. They may use the Answer Key when they finish.

SEQUENCE OF EVENTS

Introductory Lesson

Objectives:

Children will be able to remember the sequence of a story previously read.

Children will be able to correctly organize the sequence of a story not previously read.

Materials Needed:

chalkboard
ditto master
ditto paper
posterboard
scissors
felt-tipped pen

Introduction:

Tell the following story while drawing the lines as shown.

SUGGESTION: Practice telling and drawing the story before telling it to your class.

Teddy the Tug

(1) Bobby and Cindy hurried down to the harbor.

|

(2) They were excited because a great ship was due in today. They quickly walked along the dock, straining their eyes to be the first ones to see the great ship.

L__

(3) They weren't watching where they were going, and Bobby fell off the dock and into the water!

L_,

(4) Cindy screamed and several people came running. Two of the people had life preservers and threw them in the water, but they landed a long way from Bobby. Just then, a sailor dove in and pulled him over to a small boat that was tied up to a large ship.

(5) The sailor then rowed the small boat over to a dock with a ladder.

(6) Bobby and the sailor climbed up the ladder to find Cindy and a whole group of people waiting for them. Several of the people had towels and wrapped them around Bobby and the sailor.

(7) As they were drying off, they heard a loud whistle and looked out to the harbor. Far off they could see the large ship.

(8) It was being brought in very slowly by a little tugboat.

(9) When it finally reached the dock, a band was playing on one of the decks and the people on the ship were throwing confetti and long streamers. Just then a puff of wind caught one of the streamers; it went around in a circle and finally landed on the little tugboat. And here is the little tugboat!

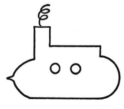

Now have the class retell the story while you follow the lines on the chalkboard drawing. After they do this, erase the drawing and ask the students to tell the story to themselves while drawing the tugboat on a sheet of paper.

Procedure:

Tell the children they are going to play a game. Prior to this you must copy each part of the following story on a sheet of posterboard. Do not include the number with each story part.

1. "Wow, look at that line of cars waiting to get in!" exclaimed Roger. Roger and his two friends, Tony and Bob, were on their way to the county fair.

2. "It's a good thing that we walked," said Bob as they made their way past the cars waiting in line.

3. "Yeah," echoed Tony. "And you wanted to ask your parents to bring us."

4. "Well, I didn't think it would be so crowded," replied Roger as the boys walked through the main gate to the fair.

5. As soon as the boys were inside the fairgrounds they made their way to the midway.

6. There were so many things to do at the midway that they just stood and stared for a short while. They didn't know what they should do first.

7. "Let's go on the Astro-Wheel," said Bob excitedly. This was a giant Ferris wheel, and the three boys quickly bought tickets and were soon high above the fairgrounds.

8. "Gosh, I didn't think this ride went up so high!" said Tony. "You can see the entire fairgrounds from up here."

9. "Look over there," said Roger as he pointed to the fun house. "Let's go in that next."

10. That sounded like a good idea to Tony and Bob so as soon as they were off the Astro-Wheel they went to the fun house.

11. When they entered the fun house, a blast of air shot up from the floor. Tony let out a yelp, and the boys stood there laughing.

12. Then they turned a corner and walked into a room that was lined with mirrors.

13. Some of the mirrors made the boys look very tall and some mirrors made them look short and fat. Tony called for the others to come and look at him. When they came and looked, the three boys broke into laughter at the sight of a "two-ton Tony"!

14. As they were leaving the fun house, Bob said, "I'm hungry!"
"Me too," chimed in Tony.

15. "Hmmmm..." said Roger. "I smell pizza!" Right next to the fun house there was a tent that served pizza. Each of the boys bought a slice and continued walking down the midway.

16. Before the boys went home they had been on almost every ride and had eaten what seemed to be tons of food.

17. "Do you think we can come back tomorrow?" asked Tony.

18. "I sure hope so," answered Roger.

19. Sure enough, the next day at ten o'clock in the morning the boys were on their way back to the fair.

Now explain to the children that you will read them a short story and they are to listen to it very carefully. Read the story in the proper order as listed above. When you finish this story, pass out the story sections that you copied on the sheets of posterboard.

> NOTE: If you have more students than story parts, simply pair up the students per story part.

The students attempt to read through the story using their story sections without getting the sequence mixed up. The student who has the beginning story section should read it aloud. The student with the next story section continues reading the story aloud, and so on until the story is finished.

> SUGGESTION: Keep a record of the errors that the students make in the sequence and discuss them afterward. After the discussion, the students might like to trade story sections and try rereading the story.

Evaluation:

Use the activity sheet "The Flower Garden" to see how well your students understand story sequence. Before distributing the activity sheet, print the following sentences on a chalkboard or transparency:

> I went so high I got scared.
>
> Mom took me to the park.
>
> Then we went home.
>
> She pushed me on the swing.

Read each of these sentences to your students. Explain that the sentences will tell a short story if they are placed in the correct order. Using the students' suggestions, place numerals next to the sentences to show the order in which they should appear. (See the Answer Key.)

```
               ANSWER KEY

  (1) Mom took me to the park.

  (2) She pushed me on the swing.

  (3) I went so high I got scared.

  (4) Then we went home.
```

Name _____

Date _____

THE FLOWER GARDEN

Here is a story about two boys who are busy making a garden. It has eight sentences, each one on a different flower. These sentences are mixed-up. You are to place them in the correct story order by numbering them. The first one has been done for you.

"Hi," hollered Keith. "Look in the sack of seeds my Dad bought for us."

He and Keith were going to plant a garden.

As soon as he had breakfast, Jim hurried to Keith's house.

It was Saturday and Jim was excited.

Keith was already outside and digging when Jim arrived.

"It's going to be a very nice garden," said Jim.

Jim looked in the sack and found five different kinds of flower seeds.

They were going to dig it behind Keith's house.

When you think your students understand the procedure, pass out the activity sheet and let them begin. Take note of those children having difficulty and plan a special group session to reteach story sequence.

The activity sheet contains eight sentences in jumbled order. As shown in the Answer Key, the sentences will form a story if the students arrange them in the correct sequence.

ANSWER KEY

(1) It was Saturday and Jim was excited.

(2) He and Keith were going to plant a garden.

(3) They were going to dig it behind Keith's house.

(4) As soon as he had breakfast, Jim hurried to Keith's house.

(5) Keith was already outside and digging when Jim arrived.

(6) "Hi," hollered Keith. "Look in the sack of seeds my Dad bought for us."

(7) Jim looked in the sack and found five different kinds of flower seeds.

(8) "It's going to be a very nice garden," said Jim.

Bulletin Boards/Displays for Skill Reinforcement

The following bulletin boards and displays have been designed to provide the students with meaningful practice in remembering story sequence.

Display Number One: A Log of Frogs

Materials Needed:

background paper
felt-tipped pens (various colors)
construction paper
paper plates
scissors
stapler
library-book card pocket
ditto master
ditto paper

Construction Directions:

1. Use an opaque projector to trace the lettering and figures onto the background paper.

2. Fold each paper plate and cut as shown here for a flatter fold.

fold   cut into both
                                                              sides on fold
                                                              about 1″

3. Attach these to the board and then use an opaque projector to trace the frogs on the background paper.

4. Print each of the following sentences on the inside of a different mouth. Follow correct letter sequence, however, from A to F. Do not follow the sequence shown here.

   C. "Let's go swimming!" called Freddie the Frog.

   D. "That sounds like fun," said his friend Flossy.

   A. The two frogs jumped into the pond.

   F. They swam over to the edge of the pond.

   E. "Now let's sun ourselves," said Flossy.

   B. "Okay," agreed Freddie as they hopped onto the shore.

5. Duplicate copies of the following:

A LOG OF FROGS
1. _____
2. _____
3. _____
4. _____
5. _____
6. _____
A - ____   D - ____
B - ____   E - ____
C - ____   F - ____

A LOG OF FROGS

Directions:

1. Take one of the sheets out of the pocket.
2. Now read the sentences inside the frogs' mouths.
3. Decide on the correct order so that they form a short story. Write the sentences in the correct order on the sheet.
4. You may use the Answer Key when you finish.

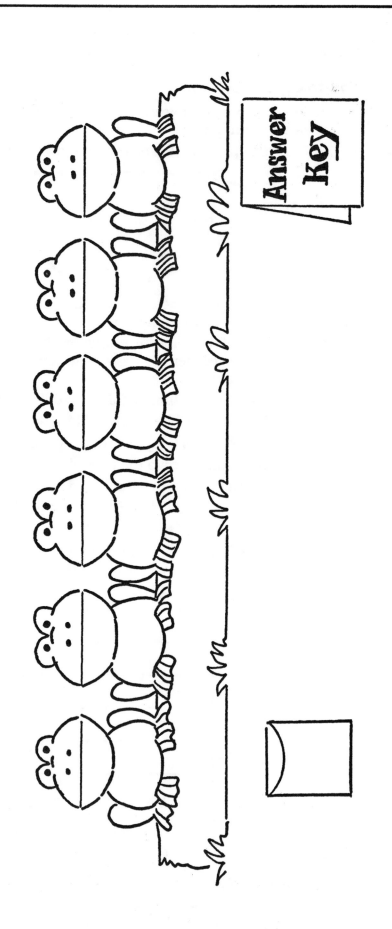

Answer Key

© 1998 by The Center for Applied Research in Education

6. Attach the card pocket on the board and place a supply of "A Log of Frogs" sheets in it.

7. Fold a sheet of construction paper and mark Answer Key on the cover. Copy the following on the inside and attach to the board:

    A – 3

    B – 6

    C – 1

    D – 2

    E – 5

    F – 4

Bulletin Board Use:

The children are to read the sentences on the board and attempt to list them in their correct story order. They do this by using the sheets on the board. When they are finished, they may use the Answer Key.

Display Number Two: Up, Up, and Away!

Materials Needed:

white background paper

felt-tipped pens (various colors)

bright-color cloth material

8 library-book card pockets

construction paper

posterboard

legal-size envelope

stapler

scissors

Construction Directions:

1. Use an opaque projector to trace the lettering and figures onto the background paper. Do not trace the balloon or title letters.

2. Cut out the title letters and balloon from the cloth material and attach to the board. You may want to use the letter patterns.

3. Attach the card pockets to the board and mark numerals on each as shown in the illustration.

4. Cut and mark the posterboard using the following balloon pattern:

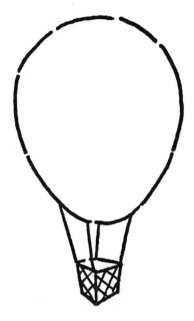

5. Copy each of the following sentences, not the numerals, on a different posterboard balloon:

    (1) "Hurry up!" shouted Ted.

    (2) "I am hurrying!" answered Jane.

    (3) Ted didn't want to be late for the air show; that is why he was hurrying Jane.

    (4) "Oh look," said Jane as they neared the gate. "There is a hot-air balloon."

    (5) Just as they went through the gate the balloon lifted off the ground.

    (6) As the balloon rose Ted said, "Look! There are two people in the basket."

    (7) The higher the balloon rose the smaller it became.

    (8) Finally it disappeared behind a cloud.

6. Print "balloons" on the envelope, attach it to the board and place the balloons in it.

7. Fold the construction paper and mark "Answer Key" on the front. Copy the numerals and sentences, in step number five, on the inside and attach it to the board.

Bulletin Board Use:

The children take the balloons out of the envelope and attempt to arrange the sentences in the correct order. They place them in the correct pockets on the bulletin board. They can check their work by looking at the Answer Key.

UP, UP, UP, AND AWAY!

Directions:

1. Take the balloons out of the envelope.
2. Read through the sentences and decide which one is the first in the short story.
3. Place this one in the first pocket in the balloon's path.
4. Continue doing the same with all the balloons.
5. You may use the Answer Key when you finish.

balloons

Answer Key

8

7

6

5

4

3

2

1

Up 'n' d
A a w
y !

Display Number Three: A Fine Catch

Materials Needed:

blue background paper
black crepe paper
felt-tipped pens (various colors)
stapler
scissors
legal-size envelope
posterboard
hole punch
straight pins
paper clips
construction paper

Construction Directions:

1. Use an opaque projector to trace the lettering and figures onto the background paper.
2. Cut the black crepe paper as shown, unfold it, and attach the "net" to the board.

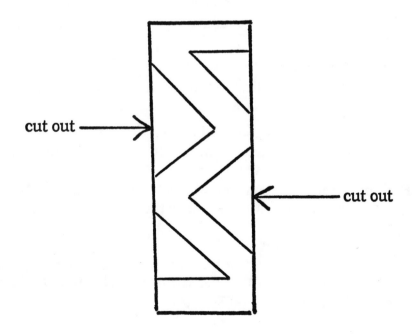

3. Attach the straight pins as shown in the board illustration.
4. Cut and mark the posterboard using the fish pattern shown here. You will need six.

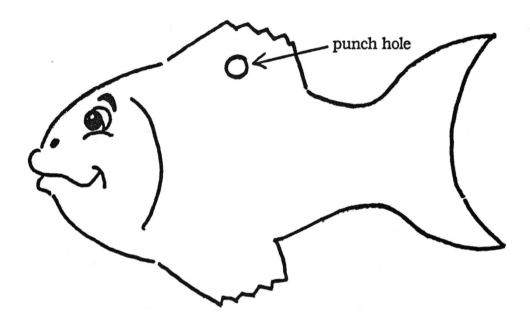

punch hole

5. Print the following sentences each on a different fish:

   Mark and Tim left to go fishing.

   They walked to the river.

   When they got there they baited their hooks.

   Tim was the first to drop his hook into the water.

   The boys waited for a bite.

   Mark jerked his pole and caught the first fish.

6. Mark "fish" on the envelope, attach it to the board and place the fish in it.
7. Fold the construction paper and mark "Answer Key" on the front. Copy the sentences in step number five on the inside and attach to the board.

Bulletin Board Use:

The children take the fish out of the envelope and place them in the correct story sequence. They are to hook them on the board in that order. When they finish, they may use the Answer Key.